NOT A TAME GOD

Christ in the Writings of C. S. Lewis

STEVEN P. MUELLER

CPH

SAINT LOUIS

To Nina

Photo of C. S. Lewis on page 2 is used by permission of The Marion E. Wade Center, Wheaton College, Wheaton, IL.

See Acknowledgments (page 7) for permissions information concerning quotations from the works of C. S. Lewis.

Scripture quotations taken from the HOLY BIBLE, NEW INTERNATIONAL VERSION®. NIV®. Copyright © 1973, 1978, 1984 by International Bible Society. Used by permission of Zondervan Publishing House. All rights reserved.

Copyright © 2002 Steven P. Mueller
Published by Concordia Publishing House
3558 S. Jefferson Avenue, St. Louis, MO 63118-3968
Manufactured in the United States of America

Library of Congress Cataloging-in-Publication Data

Mueller, Steven P., 1964–
    Not a tame God : Christ in the writings of C. S. Lewis / Steven P. Mueller.
        p.   cm.
Includes bibliographical references.
    ISBN 0-570-05296-3
    1. Jesus Christ—History of doctrines—20th century. 2. Lewis, C. S. (Clive Staples), 1898–1963—Religion. I. Title.
    BT198.M79 2002
    232'.092—dc21
                            2002003383

1 2 3 4 5 6 7 8 9 10   11 10 09 08 07 06 05 04 03 02

NOT A TAME GOD

Contents

Acknowledgments

The following books are copyrighted by the C. S. Lewis Company. All rights reserved. Quotations are used with permission.

The Four Loves by C. S. Lewis, copyright © C. S. Lewis Pte. Ltd., 1960.

God in the Dock by C. S. Lewis, copyright © C. S. Lewis Pte. Ltd., 1970.

The Great Divorce by C. S. Lewis, copyright © C. S. Lewis Pte. Ltd., 1946.

A Grief Observed by C. S. Lewis, copyright © C. S. Lewis Pte. Ltd., 1961.

The Horse and His Boy by C. S. Lewis, copyright © C. S. Lewis Pte. Ltd., 1954.

The Last Battle by C. S. Lewis, copyright © C. S. Lewis Pte. Ltd., 1956.

Letters of C. S. Lewis by C. S. Lewis, copyright © C. S. Lewis Pte. Ltd., 1966.

The Lion, the Witch and the Wardrobe by C. S. Lewis, copyright © C. S. Lewis Pte. Ltd., 1950.

Mere Christianity by C. S. Lewis, copyright © C. S. Lewis Pte. Ltd., 1942, 1943, 1944, 1952.

Miracles by C. S. Lewis, copyright © C. S. Lewis Pte. Ltd., 1947, 1960.

Perelandra by C. S. Lewis, copyright © C. S. Lewis Pte. Ltd., 1944.

The Problem of Pain by C. S. Lewis, copyright © C. S. Lewis Pte. Ltd., 1940.

The Screwtape Letters by C. S. Lewis, copyright © C. S. Lewis Pte. Ltd., 1942.

The Silver Chair by C. S. Lewis, copyright © C. S. Lewis Pte. Ltd., 1953.

Surprised by Joy by C. S. Lewis, copyright © C. S. Lewis Pte. Ltd., 1955.

That Hideous Strength by C. S. Lewis, copyright © C. S. Lewis Pte. Ltd., 1945.

Till We Have Faces by C. S. Lewis, copyright © C. S. Lewis Pte. Ltd., 1956.

The Voyage of the Dawn Treader by C. S. Lewis, copyright © C. S. Lewis Pte. Ltd., 1952.

ACKNOWLEDGMENTS

A great many people have made contributions to this work through their collegiality, scholarship, friendship, and support. I owe a debt of gratitude to dedicated professors and mentors who guided me toward this project. To Dr. Charles Manske and Dr. Rod Rosenbladt of Christ College/Concordia University, Irvine, California, who first introduced me to the scholarly study of C. S. Lewis. To Dr. David Scaer, Professor Kurt Marquart, Dr. William Weinrich, and Dr. Arthur Just of Concordia Theological Seminary, Fort Wayne, Indiana, for their guidance in my deepening research. To Dr. Ann Loades of Durham University, who through her insightful scholarship broadened my understanding and pushed me to a greater mastery and understanding of this topic.

I am grateful to the members of Redeemer Lutheran Church, Sioux City, Iowa, who allowed their pastor the time to begin this project. I am especially thankful for The Rev. Paul Sieveking, my brother in the pastoral ministry, who was a great blessing in friendship, encouragement, and advice.

This book would never have been written without the support of my colleagues and friends with whom I am privileged to serve at Concordia University, Irvine, California. They served me well as excellent teachers and encourage me today as cherished colleagues. I am indebted to the faculty of the School of Theology who challenge me, sharpen my thinking, and generously share their insights and talents. I am thankful for the literary reflections of Professor Katharine Borst; for Dr. Kerri Thomsen's literary insights, especially her thoughtful reading and response to this manuscript; and for Professor Diane Gaylor's invaluable assistance in research. I am grateful to Mr. Chris Harris for his encouragement and reactions to this book.

The Rev. Ken Wagener has been, and continues to be, a blessing through his insight, editorial work, and direction. I am thankful to the kind staff of The Marion E. Wade Center for their support in providing research materials. My gratitude also is due to the many people who have studied, reflected on, and discussed the works of C. S. Lewis with me. Here I particularly thank my students and the insightful contributors to the MereLewis e-mail listserve.

Finally, I am deeply grateful to my family for their love, support, and strength. My wife, Nina, has been a great blessing to me and has helped to shape and focus this book. My sons, Matthew, Christopher, and Jacob, helped keep me sane during its writing and honored me by allowing me to read them the stories of C. S. Lewis.

Truly the Lord has blessed me through all of these individuals and through many other friends and colleagues who also helped along the way. I am grateful to them all.

Introduction

C. S. Lewis was one of Christianity's strongest defenders in the twentieth century. In his own lifetime, he was a popular writer, and that popularity has steadily increased since his death in 1963. Today, both popular and academic books often quote his writings. He has been the subject of numerous books and articles; his life has been depicted in plays, on television, and in a movie. Stage and screen adaptations of his works have been made and continue to be produced. The majority of his books remain in print, demonstrating that his logical arguments for the truth of Christianity and his fictional narratives remain in public favor.

Lewis spent his early childhood years in a Christian home in Northern Ireland. When his mother died shortly before his 10th birthday, his father sent him to boarding school in England, where before long he rejected Christianity. The young atheist completed his education, served in World War I, and soon distinguished himself as a professor at Oxford University. During this relatively stable time of his life, at the age of 33, Lewis became a Christian again. His conversion changed everything. He began to use his literary skills to answer questions about Christianity that he had previously raised. Within two years, he combined his rediscovered faith with his professional literary abilities to publish *The Pilgrim's Regress*, a book that allegorically describes his conversion and defends Christianity. Other books followed. Lewis's years as an atheist shaped his later writings and defense of Christianity. He acknowledged his earlier objections and offered solutions that he found helpful. Readers quickly responded to this intelligent Christian witness, and they continue to do so today.

This widespread popularity and theological influence probably would have surprised Lewis. He was a layman whose academic and professional expertise was in philosophy and literature. While Lewis repeatedly reminds his writers that he is "just a layman," he frequently assumes the role of a theologian. Lewis was unwilling to leave theology to professional theologians or clergy. In *Mere Christianity*, he says that hc had been urged to present his readers with practical religious advice instead of theology. He rejected this counsel, believing that even an ordinary Christian reader would want to have a clear and accurate knowledge of God. Theology, the "science of God," is the concern of all Christians.[1]

What most distinguishes Lewis's work is his ability to communicate Christian theology. He used his talents as a teacher and speaker to explain difficult theological issues. He described the resulting writings as translations. They did not contain novel content but simply made theology more intelligible and accessible to laypeople. When this work was questioned, he responded that it was essential, saying,

> One thing at least is sure. If the real theologians had tackled this laborious work of translation about a hundred years ago, when they began to lose touch with the people (for whom Christ died), there would have been no place for me.[2]

Lewis's experience as an atheist taught him that this work was essential, and his classical and literary education gave him both the ability to understand theology and the creativity to express it in a fresh manner. He was the perfect candidate for this work of translation.

While Lewis did not claim to be a theologian, his Christian writings must be assessed on theological grounds. Whatever he intended, he did produce Christian theology and is often read as a theologian. The theological content and effectiveness of his work must be evaluated. This is particularly necessary in the central teachings of Christianity, and nothing is more central than Christology. How does Lewis understand and depict the person and work of Jesus Christ? This book will examine Lewis's writings to answer this question.

What emerges in Lewis's writings is a God who is beyond all human expectations or limitations. We might want a God that we can control or manipulate, but that would not be God at all. Lewis presents a God who is untamable but who amazingly chooses to become incarnate as a human being to save the world through His death and resurrection. In short, Lewis presents the Christ of Scripture, but he does so in fresh and creative writing.

Lewis wrote books in a variety of styles and genres. Because they present Christian theology in different ways, we will consider them according to their genre. First, we will consider his apologetic works. These books directly present Christian theology and present an apology, or defense, of Christian teaching against critics. These books include *The Problem of Pain*, *Mere Christianity*, and *Miracles*. Second, we will consider his fictional writings, namely, the Space Trilogy, *The Dark Tower*, *The Screwtape Letters*, *The Great Divorce*, the Chronicles of Narnia, and *Till We Have Faces*. These fictional works do not seek to defend Christianity, but they do present theological themes through imaginative stories. The third category of his works includes *Reflections on the Psalms*, *The Four Loves*, and *Letters to Malcolm*. These nonfictional works do not have the defensive intent or tone of his apologetics, yet they present his ideas on Christianity clearly. Because Lewis considered them as candid, devotional reflections on the Christian faith, we will classify them as devotional works. The final category includes his personal writings. Among these writings are autobiographical works, including *The Pilgrim's Regress*, which is an allegorical account of his conversion; a more traditional autobiography, *Surprised by Joy*; and a journal he kept following the death of his wife, *A Grief Observed*. His diaries and correspondence will also be considered with the personal writings.

Following this examination, Lewis's Christology will be evaluated. Because he wanted to present basic Christian theology, we will compare what he says to the ecumenical creeds. Lewis saw the creeds as a summary of Christianity and frequently alluded to them. For this reason, they form a suitable standard for evaluation. Finally, Lewis's effectiveness and weaknesses will be considered. While some critics have been reluctant to evaluate Lewis's work on theological grounds, it will stand up to scrutiny. Lewis presents a Christology that is solidly grounded in Scripture and presents the faith of the Christian church. He translates that faith to modern readers, showing us a God who is not tamed by His creatures but who surprises us with His endless grace.

NOTES

1. C. S. Lewis, *Mere Christianity* (New York: Macmillan, 1952), 135.
2. C. S. Lewis, "Rejoinder to Dr. Pittenger," in *God in the Dock: Essays on Theology and Ethics*, ed Walter Hooper (New York: Macmillan, 1970), 103.

Chapter One

The Problem of Pain

One of the most difficult issues that Christians face is the existence of pain and suffering. Why does it exist? Why doesn't God end all suffering? Does He have the power to stop it? What does the existence of suffering have to say about the existence, goodness, or power of God? These are difficult questions, even in an abstract sense, but they are far more difficult when they relate directly to our personal experiences. It is easy to speak philosophically about pain, but it is difficult to endure it.

Because these questions are a stumbling block for many people, Lewis addressed them directly in *The Problem of Pain*, the first of his apologetic works. As in many of his books, he demonstrates a willingness to leave questions unresolved, if necessary. Before giving in, however, he struggles to make sense of these issues. To do this, he applies both theology and philosophy to the problem of pain, striving not for innovation or novelty but for clarity. His goal is not to create new theology but to explain classic orthodoxy and apply time-tested principles to this issue. Lewis acknowledges his weaknesses, using them as a defense against theological criticism. He candidly notes that he is not a professional theologian or a member of the clergy; rather, he is "a layman and an amateur." At the same time, he strove to be faithful to historic Christianity. In fact, he claims that with the exception of the chapters on the suffering of animals and on heaven, the majority of *The Problem of Pain* is simply a restatement of orthodox Christian teaching.[1]

Lewis clearly intends to be faithful to orthodox Christianity. The question, of course, is whether he is successful. Lewis may have intended to write as a layman and an amateur, but his works are often read theologically.

The primary focus of this book is on pain. Lewis considers this to be a philosophical question with theological significance as well. Because of this focus, we would not expect to find much material specifically on Christology. Surprisingly, a great deal of Lewis's theology emerges as he considers the problem of pain. In this work, Lewis addresses the person and work of Christ and the work of the atonement, applying all of these to our human suffering.

THE DEITY OF CHRIST

Our first encounter with Christ in *The Problem of Pain* comes in assertions of His divinity. While the deity of Christ is not particularly germane to Lewis's discussion of pain, it is assumed and explained with doctrinal precision. For example, Lewis notes that God's self-identification as Father is also an expression of His goodness. The Father and the Son exist in a unique relationship in which the Son exhibits complete submission and perfect obedience. As this is described, however, Lewis inserts a parenthetical remark regarding an essential divergence between God and earthly fathers and sons. The divine Son is united with His Father and, like His Father, has existed for all eternity. While this is a logical and temporal impossibility for human beings, it is not impossible for God.[2]

Unity and coeternity with the Father are presented as an assumption of our faith. Lewis does not defend these doctrinal statements here. Instead, having identified his orthodox position, he proceeds with the main point of this passage—that fatherly authority and filial obedience are exemplified in the relationship between the First and Second Persons of the Trinity.

This theme of obedience returns in, "Human Pain," the central chapter of the book. Here Lewis narrows the definition of pain to be synonymous with suffering. He maintains that suffering may come from a refusal to submit to our Creator. This submission is not difficult when the creatures see it to be in their own interest, though they are often blinded to this realization. Many consider submission to be a difficult, even impossible, task. In response, Lewis highlights the submission of the Son to the Father. The Second Person of the Trinity, who is eternally begotten of His Father, exhibits perfect love for His Father. He selflessly gives Himself back to His Father in full and joyful obedience to the Father's will. Lewis considers this shared love to be so strong and vibrant that it is, in fact, the Third Person of the Trinity. Thus, love and obedience are the pattern of reality. They are perfectly manifest in the Holy Trinity. The Creator made humanity to live in this same love and joyful obedience.[3] In this humble submission, the eternal Son provides the ultimate example of filial obedience.

Unfortunately, while affirming this truth, Lewis employs imprecise language regarding the Trinity. Stressing the unity of the Godhead, Lewis refers to God *"as Son"* and *"as Father."* Use of the word "as" in reference to Son and Father may imply the reduction of "person" in the Trinity to a temporary function. This is not the language of orthodoxy. The wording is imprecise, but the rest of his discussion balances the imprecision with affirmations of creedal orthodoxy. The relationship of the persons of the Trinity is on a much higher plane than any created being can imagine. Lewis clearly asserts the transcendence not only of the Father, but also of the Son. The Son is God Himself, and He is Son from all eternity. Taken in context, we see that Lewis does assume the full deity of Christ.

THE INCARNATION

While Lewis maintains the deity of the Son, he spends more time on His incarnation and humanity. The doctrine of the incarnation and its application to human struggles is not as pronounced in this book as in later writings, but Lewis does discuss it with conviction. For example, writing on "Divine Goodness," he asks whether it is appropriate to distinguish between egoistic, selfish love and altruistic love with reference to God. Lewis notes that these concepts are only relevant when beings inhabit a common world and have conflicting interests. Because God is so far above us, the categories of selfishness or unselfishness do not really apply. But this is altered in the incarnation. God takes on a life of self-sacrifice, emptying Himself of His glory and submitting to death by crucifixion.[4] The incarnation is the first incidence of true altruism that the world has ever seen. God unselfishly gives everything for us. In contrast, human lives are selfish.

The altruistic act of the incarnation unites full deity and full humanity in Jesus Christ. While Lewis emphasizes Christ's unique deity, His humanity always remains evident. This is highlighted in the struggle between the human desire to avoid suffering and the desire of the Son to please His Father. Lewis maintains that Christianity does not require a pursuit of suffering or even passivity to it. Christians, like all other people, naturally try to avoid pain. But the Christian will prefer God and His will to other ends and will not seek to escape pain at all costs. Submission to God's will may necessitate suffering. Christ models this for us in the Garden of Gethsemane. Being perfectly human, He sought to avoid His own suffering and death. This natural human desire, however, was subject to the Father's will. Suffering would not shake Christ's obedience.[5]

If Jesus had avoided suffering at all costs, He would have denied the very work He came to do. To accept pain without hesitation would be less than human. The struggle indicates that Christ is truly a human being. His perfect submission demonstrates His deity. His followers are also called to submit to God's will, but none can perfectly follow Jesus' example.

Lewis presents a high view of the incarnation. Christ is indeed the Perfect Man, but that perfection, which the rest of humanity is unable to attain, does not diminish His humanity. He is subject to human limitations. Lewis uses this limitation to explain statements Christ made that may trouble some Christians.

> [I]t might be argued that when He emptied Himself of His glory He also humbled Himself to share, as man, the current superstitions of His time. And I certainly think that Christ in the flesh was not omniscient—if only because a human brain could not, presumably, be the vehicle of omniscient consciousness, and to say that Our Lord's thinking was not really conditioned by the size and shape of His brain might be to deny the real incarnation and become a Docetist. Thus, if Our Lord had committed Himself to any scientific or historical statement which we knew to be untrue, this would not disturb my faith in His deity.[6]

Lewis limits himself to statements of Christ that seem to contradict scientific or historical facts, but he does not extend this to nonfactual opinions held by our culture. Lewis's words allow Jesus to speak in the scientific and historical context of His time without necessarily agreeing with ours. If the scientific and historical worldview has changed, this does not negate His deity. Rather, Lewis considers it an affirmation of His true humanity.

Many readers may find these thoughts challenging. It would be helpful to know more of Lewis's thoughts on the extent and meaning of the humiliation of Christ, but details are lacking here. In particular, it would be helpful to have more details concerning the relationship between the omniscience of God and the limited knowledge of human beings. Lewis here denies that Christ was omniscient in His human nature. He supports this by saying that the opposite view is that of the Docetists. Docetism was a heresy in the early church that maintained that Christ was truly God but only appeared to be human. Lewis argues that a true human nature could not be omniscient. What Lewis does not account for in these words is the power of God to overcome all limitations. While normal human beings are not omniscient, they do not possess a divine nature either. The incarnate Christ is unique.

It is interesting to note that in the French edition of *The Problem of Pain*, prepared 10 years after the book was first published in English, Lewis adds a footnote that distances himself from these words. In the French edition, he admits that his description was inadequate and revealed an ignorance of the finer points of the doctrine.[7] While we wish this footnote had been included in all editions of this book, it is encouraging to see Lewis's admission of his limitations. It would be wise to consider these words as Lewis did, as those of a layman and amateur. While he overstated his position, he was trying to make allowance for an apparent conflict of faith and reason while still upholding the full humanity and deity of Christ.

THE WORK OF CHRIST

Jesus Christ, the incarnate God, truly is without equal. Some would attribute this superiority to His teaching, but the supremacy of Christ is not the result of His teaching alone. Other great ethical teachers proclaim similar messages. History is filled with evidence of human wickedness (which is one of the main causes of pain), and there have always been teachers who have called for ethical behavior. In evidence, Lewis cites teachers who hold substantial ethical teaching (what he would later refer to as the *Tao*) in common: Zarathustra, Jeremiah, Socrates, Gautama (the Buddha), Christ, and Marcus Aurelius. A footnote on Christ explains that, unlike the rest of these teachers, He is the incarnate God. Nonetheless, it is not the teaching that distinguishes Jesus Christ. Although His teaching is important, it is not entirely innovative. Rather, what distinguishes Christ is His person—fully human, fully divine—and His office—the Savior of the world.[8]

THE ATONEMENT

One of the distinctive characteristics of C. S. Lewis's theology is a dislike of atonement theories. Atonement theories are particular ways to describe how the work of Christ is effective and to organize what the Bible says. Should Christ be described mainly as a substitute for sinners? Would it be better to call Him a ransom, and if so, who receives the ransom? Perhaps His work is better described as physical combat with Satan. These are simple examples of atonement theories. They are generally based on Scripture, but they may emphasize some Bible passages more than others. Lewis did not question the reality of Christ's work and its effectiveness in the lives of God's people, but he struggled with those who would insist on extrabiblical explanations. In particular, Lewis struggled with the Anselmic theory of the atonement, which is also known as the vicarious satisfaction. Although Lewis frequently writes against such theories, he himself easily slips into using them. Consider his presentation of the fall of man, in which he talks about Anselm's depiction of the atonement in legal terms. Lewis particularly struggled with Anselm's explanation that we are included in Christ's suffering by means of a "legal fiction."

> These theories may have done good in their day but they do no good to me, and I am not going to invent others. ... It may be that the acts and sufferings of great archetypal individuals such as Adam and Christ are ours, not by legal fiction, metaphor, or causality, but in some much deeper fashion.[9]

Lewis's main objections are that the Anselmic theory does not help him and that it explains too much. Yet he uses existing theories of the atonement in his explanations of the work of Christ. For example, writing about the inappropriateness of speaking as if sins committed in the past need not trouble the Christian, he says that the passing of time does not make these sins disappear. Only Christ's shed blood has washed away our guilt.[10]

Despite his claim not to invent new models, Lewis does speculate on the atonement. One of the more pertinent discussions involves a question of God's power. If God has almighty power, why didn't He simply remove that first sin and restore creation to its original state? Lewis answers that this would be only a temporary solution. God would have had to do the same thing for every sin that followed the first. God did not deny the reality of the sin. Instead, He decisively solved the problem of sin through Christ's death.[11]

Throughout his writings, Lewis offers his objections to atonement theories and provides his own explanations. While his thinking becomes more developed and precise, he continues to accept the reality of the atonement. He questions how it should be explained, but he does not question its truth.

A Specific Problem: The Problem of Hell

It is one thing to talk about pain in abstract issues, another to consider specific problems. For Lewis, one of the most difficult problems is the existence of hell. God is so merciful that He became human and died an agonizing death to save humanity from damnation. Why, then, does that merciful God not intervene when some of His creatures reject His salvation? Why won't He compel them to be saved?

The problem of hell, for Lewis, embraces the wonders of the work of Christ. How could a God who is willing to do so much tolerate hell? Lewis expands the problem, saying that he would pay any price to remove this doctrine. Yet any price a human being could pay would pale in comparison to what God has already paid to free us from hell. Lewis was disturbed that God has shown us so much mercy, yet there is still a hell.[12]

How can this paradox be reconciled? Ultimately for Lewis, the problem of hell, as indeed much of the problem of pain, flows from free will. Freedom includes the possibility of rejecting divine mercy. God will not force Himself upon humanity, even if that means they may reject Him. In fact, He has already done more than we could ask. We might beg Him to forgive all sins and give people a new beginning, but this has already been done. He has provided a solution to humanity's problems, but many have rejected that solution. It was not God's will that they do so, but He will not force us to receive His mercy.[13] Lewis comes to his sad conclusion by way of Christology. God has already done everything, but He will not force anyone to believe. Ultimately, if one asks to be left alone, God will regretfully comply.

CONCLUSION

Before writing this book, Lewis had experienced suffering: the death of his mother, a strained relationship with his father, wartime service, and his subsequent wounding in battle. But the greatest sufferings of his life lay before him. It was in his latter years that Lewis encountered his most profound pain and applied his understanding of suffering. As he experienced his wife's battle with cancer and mourned her death, Lewis truly faced, and dealt with, his own pain. Part of his struggle is recorded in *A Grief Observed*.

Lewis freely admitted the shortcomings of *The Problem of Pain*. For example, in a 1951 letter, [14] he answered some questions on suffering, commenting that he wished that he had known more when he wrote this book. He did not view *The Problem of Pain* as a final or authoritative answer to the question of suffering; rather, he considered it as the beginning of an answer. Likewise, it is not his definitive work on Christology, but only a portion of his Christological thinking. While *The Problem of Pain* is not about Christology, Lewis's understanding of the person and work of Christ certainly influences his view of pain. The ultimate answer to suffering is heaven, which is attained through the redemption of Jesus Christ, who knows and understands human pain, having faced it on behalf of humanity. Until salvation is attained, pain remains part of life. It may be caused by the misuse of our freedom—our poor choices—or inflicted by other people, but it is not inflicted by God.

Lewis admitted the reality of pain and the inability of human beings to remove it. He also noted that pain might be used for a greater end because it demands our attention and cries for a response. Indeed, Lewis said that pain is one of God's most effective ways to get the attention of our fallen world.[15] Pain is a part of the human experience, but it is not the whole experience. Indeed, pain may be used to good ends. Perhaps it may wake a deaf world to the reality of God's solution. Perhaps it will point to Christ.

NOTES

1. C. S. Lewis, *The Problem of Pain* (New York: Macmillan, 1962), 10.
2. Ibid., 45.
3. Ibid., 90–91.
4. Ibid., 49.
5. Ibid., 113.
6. Ibid., 134.
7. C. S. Lewis, *La Problème de la Souffrance* (Paris: Desclée de Brouwer, 1950), 163.
8. Lewis, *Problem of Pain*, 63.
9. Ibid., 86–87.
10. Ibid., 61.
11. Ibid., 71.
12. Ibid., 119–20.
13. Ibid., 128.
14. W. H. Lewis, ed. *The Letters of C. S. Lewis* (New York: Harcourt, Brace, Jovanovich, 1966), 234.
15. Lewis, *Problem of Pain*, 93.

Chapter Two

Mere Christianity

In the early 1940s, England was deeply engaged in World War II. The Nazis had relentlessly bombed London and other cities, and even when the bombing had slackened, it remained a vivid memory and a threat for the future. Shortages, hardship, and death were all too familiar. The horrors of war inevitably spawned difficult questions. Why doesn't God intervene and stop the war? Can there really be a place for Christianity within a world like this? Does it speak to our needs today, or is it hopelessly out of date, illogical, and archaic? Does Christianity have anything to offer our modern world?

In response to this crisis of faith, the BBC turned to C. S. Lewis, asking him to deliver a series of four radio addresses. He was to speak about Christianity for 15 minutes each week. When the addresses were well received, more were scheduled over a two-and-a-half-year period. In time, Lewis reedited and published them, first as three separate books, and eventually together as *Mere Christianity*.

This book is one of Lewis's most famous and influential writings. One reason for this is its scope. Again, Lewis intentionally limits his writing to teachings that are held in common by most Christian churches. These core doctrines are what he terms "mere Christianity." He does not seek to defend or promote one denomination over another, but he does proclaim our common belief to those who yet do not believe it.

Lewis tried to restrict himself to mere Christianity in most of his works, and he deferred to the "real experts" and "real theologians" when faced with challenging issues. He acknowledges that he is out of his element in the finer points of theology or church history. Articles of Christian doctrine that divide denominations can be particularly difficult to understand and explain. Aware of his limitations, Lewis focused on the common core of Christianity and left more sophisticated points to those with greater qualifications.[1] There are times when he strays from his ideal and presents more controversial theological positions, but ultimately he returns to common ground. Because of this focus on shared teaching, Lewis's writings have been well received by many different Christians.

Mere Christianity, however, does not mean *simplistic* Christianity. The Christian faith, like life itself, may initially appear more simple than it is. The truth may have greater complexity and depth than is first apparent. Lewis works to explain and reveal theology, but he does not back away from difficult teaching. He was willing to examine Christianity logically, but he remained reliant on divine revelation. This reliance may lead to complexity, but it is the complexity of truth. He was certain that an intelligent reader would want to be challenged by the depth of mature faith, rather than settling for simplistic teachings.[2]

Lewis treats his readers as he would like to be treated. If he could study and appreciate theology, so could other ordinary Christians. Clearly a book written for a lay reader would have a different character than one written primarily for theologians, but the topics need not be vastly different. Lewis believed that any Christian could understand and might want to understand Christian theology.

Lewis takes the time to explain and illustrate theology to the reader. He seeks out new analogies, descriptions, and formulations to clarify his belief, yet his descriptions are not particularly lengthy. As his radio addresses covered topics in 15 minutes, his chapters briefly address theological issues. Within a few minutes, the reader can explore a significant theological topic.

PREPARING FOR CHRIST

Because there is nothing more essential to Christianity than the person and work of Jesus Christ, Lewis spends considerable time on our Savior. Yet this is not his starting place. He begins by seeking common ground with his readers by exploring universal concepts of right and wrong. Although many people make no attempt to act in accordance with these concepts, they demonstrate their belief that they exist whenever they plead for their rights or for fairness. Lewis suggests that these principles are part of an underlying order to the universe. The prevalence of this common morality might be seen as the work of a supernatural being or reality.[3] Failure to live according to these principles produces guilt. Lewis has now completed his preparation for the Christian message. He has given evidence of a universal moral law and asserted that there is a supernatural power behind that law. Because we have broken the law, we find ourselves at odds with that supernatural power. The Christian message is a response to this problem. Now the reader is prepared to hear the Gospel.[4]

The reader might expect Lewis immediately to begin presenting Christ, but he does not do this. Instead, he highlights four specific aspects of God's response. First, he reminds us again that God gave human beings a conscience. Throughout history, people have tried, unsuccessfully, to follow their consciences.[5] The conscience testifies to the existence of God and His will. Second, Lewis maintains that God responds to our human condition through paganism and its myths. He is particularly interested in the many myths that depict a god who dies and returns to life again to give life to humanity.[6] This is one of the more distinctive marks of Lewis's theology. Lewis firmly believed that the pagan myths were part of God's revelation. They are not a substitute for the Gospel, nor are they an end in themselves. Rather, they serve to prepare people for Christ by revealing the possibility of a dying and rising God.

Moreover, in response to our human condition, God selected one particular people, the Jews. He taught them about Himself. He showed them that despite these pagan myths, there was only one true God. He taught them that He cared about their conduct. His revelation was more specific with the Jews than it was through the human conscience or paganism. Yet all three of these steps were preparatory. They met their fulfillment with God's fourth response: the coming of the Christ.

GOD'S RESPONSE IN CHRIST

Finally, in fulfillment of His plan, God sent Jesus. Lewis begins his examination of Jesus by looking at His own testimony. Here we see a God who will not be tamed or confined by human limitations. Jesus shatters our expectations and challenges us by claiming to be divine. He asserted His authority to forgive sins, spoke as if He had always existed, and stated that He would return to judge the world. Taken in context, Jesus' words are unbelievably shocking.[7] The Gospels are clear: Jesus claimed to be God. Because Jesus Himself made these claims, we cannot ignore them. Yet people often try to ignore them or explain them away. Might Jesus have been simply an important person, a good man, or a moral teacher, but not divine? Lewis responds that such explanations cannot be reconciled with Christ's claims about Himself.

> A man who was merely a man and said the sort of things Jesus said would not be a great moral teacher. He would either be a lunatic—on a level with the man who says he is a poached egg—or else he would be the Devil of Hell. You must make your choice. Either this man was, and is, the Son of God: or else a madman or something worse. You can shut Him up for a fool, you can spit at Him and kill Him as a demon; or you may fall at His feet and call Him Lord and God. But let us not come with any patronising nonsense about His being a great human teacher. He has not left that open to us. He did not intend to.[8]

Lewis is not addressing every possibility of Christ's identity. He is writing against one particular hypothesis: that Jesus was merely a good teacher. In arguing against this position, Lewis has distilled the possibilities to three. He does not, in this context, provide a more detailed examination of these options, but before moving on, he concludes that it is evident that Jesus was neither a lunatic nor a devil. The only remaining option is that Jesus' claims are true: He is the incarnate God.[9] Despite this logical examination, however, Lewis does not impose his conclusion on his readers. He states his conclusion more winsomely, saying that these things are obvious to him. Lewis draws a logical conclusion, believing that Jesus is divine, and hopes that others will follow his logic to this same understanding.

Christ's Humanity

The timeless, only-begotten Son of God shockingly chose to become human. The untamable God willingly became part of His creation, subject to the actions of His creatures. This is not a theological abstraction. Lewis makes the incarnation as specific as possible. The God who created humanity by His power chose to take on a human nature. He did not merely give the outward appearance of humanity, but He actually became human. As such, He took on particular human characteristics: a specific height, weight, and hair color. He lived among a specific people and spoke their language. This change is unfathomably drastic.

> The Eternal Being, who knows everything and who created the whole universe, became not only a man but (before that) a baby, and before that a *fœtus* inside a Woman's body. If you want to get the hang of it, think how you would like to become a slug or a crab.[10]

God became a specific, historical human being. The limitless God took on a real human nature. Even in the womb, Christ was the incarnate Son of God. Lewis could have taken this further. He might have taken this back to the conception of Christ. Instead, he appears to leave some latitude for the precise moment the incarnation begins. Of far more importance, in Lewis's view, was the significance of incarnation. This is no minor event; it shows the extent of God's love for us. Lewis invites the reader to consider the drastic nature of the incarnation. Almighty God willingly humbled Himself and became a human being for our sake. He became human to suffer and die for us.

The Son became a real human being, deriving His human nature from His mother. Ordinary biological growth and nurture sustained His life. Yet the incarnation does not mean that God became something less than He was before. Echoing the language of the Athanasian Creed, Lewis writes that the incarnation does not lower the divine nature; instead, it ennobles the human nature. The goal of the incarnation was the redemption of a fallen humanity, but it also affirmed the primal goodness of God's creation of humanity.[11]

While showing Christ's true humanity, Lewis states that the human nature was turned into the begotten life. This does not mean, however, that the human nature ceased to exist. Both natures are inseparably joined together for all eternity. This is particularly reflected in the resurrection. While a human nature does not ordinarily rise from the dead, both natures in Christ rose, not only the divine. Even now, the resurrected Christ remains the God-man: perfectly human and perfectly divine.

While He is fully human, Christ is not simply another ordinary man. He is the archetype of the new humanity, *the* new man who gives life to all humans. Christ takes on a human nature so He might give life to all humanity. He is the only one who is, by nature, the true Son of God, but His work allows other humans to become the children of God.[12]

Christ was truly a human being, like us in every way but one. He was without sin. Lewis stresses this point, suggesting the intriguing idea that bad people really know very little about badness because they always succumb to temptation. They have led a sheltered life and consequently do not learn the full extent of evil. Because we so readily give in, we do not really know the strength of our sinful nature nor the extent of Satan's temptation. We begin to see this power when we try to resist our sinful desires. Often, we do not even try to resist. In contrast, Christ never yielded to temptation. Consequently, He faced a degree of temptation that we have never experienced. Not only was He tempted as we are, He faced even stronger temptations.[13]

Christ is sinless, yet He has undergone temptation. This is consistent with the biblical accounts, yet it is Lewis's unique emphasis that resistance gives Christ a full knowledge of temptation. This knowledge is not the result of omniscience, it is a result of experience.

CHRIST AND THE TRINITY

A further aspect of Christ's nature is His relationship to the Trinity. Scripture teaches that there is only one God, yet the Father, Son, and Holy Spirit are called God. Lewis has demonstrated that Christ Himself claimed to be God and the only logical understanding of His claims is to believe them. While this teaching is central to the Christian faith, orthodox Christianity has maintained that this doctrine is a mystery that is beyond human understanding. Because of this, extensive explanations can be misleading. Analogies and illustrations are useful, but only to a limited degree. As Lewis attempts to explain the Trinity, he does so with mixed success. He focuses primarily on the Father and the Son, with less time spent on the Holy Spirit. In addition to biblical texts, Lewis looks to individual experience and the corporate experience of the church for explanations of the Trinity.

One way that Lewis explains the doctrine of the Trinity is by considering the experience of the individual Christian in prayer. This description is not designed to give an orderly doctrinal presentation, but it brings that doctrine closer to the individual Christian. Lewis is assuming that his readers are already aware of the doctrine of the Trinity. He writes to show them a way that they experience the Trinity each day.

The experience of prayer reveals God to Lewis on multiple levels. As a Christian prays, prayers are addressed to God. Through Scripture, we learn, however, that it is not our own impulse that moves us to pray. Rather, God, who dwells within us (the Holy Spirit), motivates our prayers. At the same time, we know that Christ, the incarnate God, also helps us pray and, indeed, is constantly interceding for us.[14] Without using trinitarian language, Lewis has presented the entire Trinity. Clearly, He is envisioning prayers addressed to the Father. The Holy Spirit, God within us, prompts and enables our prayers. So also Christ enables our prayers and continues to pray for us. In this description, the clearest revelation of divinity takes place in Jesus Christ. In contrast, the other two persons are harder to conceptualize. Lewis is trying to provide an orthodox view of the Trinity, yet by avoiding the specific names of the Father and the Spirit, he invites misunderstanding. He has brought the work of the Trinity into the daily life of Christians through their experience. Taken alone, however, this illustration is prone to misapplication.

While the prayers of an individual Christian might suggest the doctrine of the Trinity, it becomes more pronounced in the collective experience of the Christian church. Here Lewis's understanding of the Trinity is seen with greater clarity. It is evident that he considered the formulation of this doctrine to be a development of the early church. Believers had already known about God, though their knowledge was incomplete and even vague. Then

31

they encountered Jesus, who said that He was God. There was no easy way to avoid His claims. He clearly meant what He said, and He was not a lunatic. They had to consider the truthfulness of His claims. Furthermore, His resurrection from the dead reinforced their belief. Jesus was truly God. Lewis sees the final development of the doctrine of the Trinity in the early church. As the believers gather together, they also find God present inside of them. When the early Christians had combined these three things, they arrived at the doctrine of the Trinity. This, according to Lewis, was the beginning of theology.[15]

Note how this depiction of the Trinity is strongly focused on Christ. Humanity knew God before the incarnation, but this knowledge was vague. Awareness of Christ's deity expanded humanity's conception of God. But once again, when approaching the Holy Spirit, Lewis retreats into vagueness. Christians became aware of another presence of God, finding Him inside of themselves in some way.

Lewis's initial descriptions of the Trinity uphold the deity of all three persons but fail to properly distinguish them. He strongly emphasizes the deity of Christ and acknowledges the Father, but he is weak on the Holy Spirit. While Lewis intended to present orthodoxy, his descriptions are prone to misinterpretation. In this context, he does not indicate that the three persons are coexistent or coeternal. These descriptions, based on singular or corporate experience, fall short of the orthodoxy to which he aspired. He has tried to explain the inexplicable and failed. If these descriptions were to stand alone, this book could not be commended as orthodox. But after illustrating the doctrine of the Trinity with these imprecise statements, Lewis presents a series of trinitarian statements that draw heavily on the language of orthodoxy.

When asked to express his beliefs succinctly, Lewis often relied on the creeds. For example, as he examines the relationship of Christ to the Trinity, Lewis begins with the proposition of the Nicene Creed that "the only-begotten Son of God" was "begotten of His Father before all worlds ... begotten, not made." Discussing this ecumenical creed, Lewis first notes that this article does not refer to the virgin birth (which is confessed later in the creed). Then he states that this phrase is not describing the conception of Jesus' human nature but the origin of His divinity. The Son of God is eternally begotten of His Father, not created by Him. But what does this mean? Lewis carefully defines these concepts. A creation is something that is made, something of a different nature than the creator. In contrast, begetting does not produce something different but something of the same nature as the one from which it comes. Humans may create all manner of things, but they may only beget humans. God is the creator of all things, yet He did not create His Son. The Son is eternally begotten of His Father.[16]

The Son is the same sort of thing as the Father, not a creature but God. Even so, the Son owes His divine nature and existence to the Father. One illustration of this relationship is the familiar analogy of two books that are eternally stacked together. The upper book could not hold its position were it not for the support of the lower book, yet there never was a time when the two books were not stacked. Likewise, the Son owes His nature to the Father, but He is eternally begotten of the Father. There never was a time when the Son was not begotten. The begetting does not imply that the Father existed before the Son. We naturally want to consider the relationship of the Father and the Son in temporal terms, as we do our own human relationships. Unlike us, however, God is not bound by time. The Son owes His existence and nature to His Father, but this is true from all eternity. Both the Father and the Son are eternal. There never was a time when the Son was not begotten.[17]

In another instance, Lewis uses a geometric illustration to describe the Trinity. A cube is one shape, but it is made up of six squares joined together. Similarly, God consists of three persons but remains only one God.[18] Reversion to geometric images is a common tactic for a description of the Trinity. It is interesting, however, to note that Lewis does not use the most common picture—that of a triangle. Instead of this familiar illustration, Lewis writes of a square and a cube, incorporating the language of dimensional differentiation. A square may be part of a cube, but that does not change the fact that it is a square. Lewis uses this analogy to demonstrate an instance in which plurality and unity may coexist.

In another section, Lewis works with more abstract illustrations. The Son streams forth from the Father like light from a lamp, heat from a fire, or thoughts from a mind. Lewis employs an interesting switch of language here. "Streaming" seems like a more natural description of the procession of the Holy Spirit. At the same time, Lewis describes Christ as God's self-expression or as what the Father has to say, and even as thoughts from a mind. These comparisons reflect St. John's description of Jesus as the divine Word (*Logos*) who becomes incarnate. In each case, Lewis reminds his readers that we should imagine this "streaming forth" as an eternal reality. However, these diverse illustrations of the Trinity leave Lewis unsatisfied. Although all are illustrative, they make the Father and the Son sound like objects and not persons. In the end, Lewis returns to the biblical description of this relationship: Father and Son. This original depiction is more accurate than any substitution we humans might devise. We should expect that this would be true. God's self-revelation will inevitably be better than any depiction we might imagine. Additionally, the biblical image of God the Father and God the Son reminds us that theirs is a relationship of love.[19]

If Lewis toys with the language of procession (streaming) to describe the Son, he eventually returns to more typical expressions. He notes a strong preference for use of the biblical images over other analogies because analogies may depersonalize the Trinity. Despite all his "translation" of theology, his illustration and description, Lewis ultimately decides that the best language for description of the Godhead is the language that God has used to describe Himself. The language of Father-Son is normative because it is God's self-disclosure.

After noting that love is of prime importance to understanding, Lewis finally gets specific regarding the Third Person of the Trinity. Lewis does not use the typical language of procession of the Spirit. Instead, he writes of the love expressed between the Father and the Son. This love is so strong, so vivid, that it is a person. The Holy Spirit is, essentially, the eternal love shared between the Father and the Son.[20] We should be careful to note that this does not deny the personality of the Spirit. The Spirit remains fully God. In Lewis's description, as the Son owes His existence to the Father, so the Spirit owes His existence to the Father and the Son. In this, Lewis stands in the heritage of the Western Church, paralleling the creedal affirmation that the Spirit "proceeds from the Father and the Son."

Overall, Lewis strives to present the orthodox view of the Trinity. He relies on creedal formulations and time-honored illustrations, supplementing these with new descriptions and analogies. At times, he appears to approach error, only to return to orthodox statements of this teaching. It is ill-advised to try to explain the mystery of the Trinity. In the end, it remains a mystery that is believed. What Lewis believes and presents is that Christ is essential to the Trinity. Only through the God-man do we begin to know God as Father, Son, and Holy Spirit.

THE WORK OF CHRIST

Mere Christianity presents Christ as the incarnate God. It does not stop with His nature, but it continues with His work. It is essential to our salvation that Christ be both God and man. We are sinners who need to repent. The challenge is that while only a bad person needs to repent, only a good person is able to repent perfectly. Because of this, we cannot be saved unless something is changed. That change is seen in the work of Christ. In Christ, these two realities are brought together. The perfection of the divine nature is united in one person with a human nature. Because of this, the God-man is able to suffer and to die.[21] Jesus, who has "amalgamated" these two natures, is able to help humanity. Because He is human, He can experience our human state. He can surrender His will, suffer, and die. Because He is God, He can do it perfectly. The incarnation is essential because only in the union of these two natures could humanity's salvation be carried out. Echoing his earlier assessment of Christ's work, Lewis reminds us again that while Jesus was a teacher, this is not the heart of His work. Christianity proclaims that the primary work of Christ was His death and resurrection.

Lewis rightly believes that the redemption is Christ's chief work. Yet here Lewis stumbles in his theology. How are we to speak of what Christ does? Lewis is again addressing the topic of atonement theories, which attempt to describe how Christ's work is effective. These theories prove troublesome to Lewis throughout his writings. Are such doctrinal formulations essential? He writes that before his conversion, he believed that Christians were required to believe one particular theory—the Anselmic theory. He understood this description to say that God wanted to punish humanity for rejecting Him and following the devil. When Christ voluntarily took the punishment we deserved, God spared us, and we were saved.[22]

Lewis notes three objections to theories of the atonement. The first is that theories are not Christianity; they are explanations of how Christianity works. A person can accept that Christ has saved and delivered him without having to understand precisely how this works. In fact, he would be unable to understand it until he believed.[23] The explanation itself is unnecessary. This is a fair assessment, but it does not invalidate the theories. Lewis, who himself proposes explanations of many Christian teachings, is hardly in a position to criticize other explanations on such a level. His objections are surprising from a man who expects that the Christian will seek to know as much about God as possible. True, no one is required to consider these theories, but one would have thought Lewis would have wanted to do so. And, indeed, he does desire an examination.

His other objections to atonement theory are based on content. He has defined this theory as stating that God wanted to punish us, but Christ volunteered to be punished instead, so God forgave us. Here Lewis questions the need for Christ's death. If this was simply God's decision not to punish us, why did Christ have to die? Why didn't He just forgive us without the punishment falling on Jesus? Furthermore, he stumbles over the connection of Christ to the punishment. How is it right that an innocent person was punished? Lewis answers his own questions. What is the point of punishing an innocent person? None, if this is conceptualized in a criminal or punitive sense, as Lewis appears to do. But he immediately continues to say that it does indeed make sense when it is considered in financial terms. There is a point in someone paying the debt that another person has accumulated. A friend may choose to pay someone else's bills. Likewise, a person may choose to appear guilty and bear a penalty that another person earned. Experience has shown that friends often bear the punishment of another.

Lewis shows by these exceptions that he really does not have a problem with theories of the atonement, only with one narrow view of one theory. Lewis offers his own explanation, but true to his first objection, he notes that his explanation of the atonement is only one more picture. It is not the atonement itself but only another description of how it works. If a reader is not helped by this explanation, Lewis encourages her to ignore it.[24]

Later, we see Lewis willing to use different explanations to describe Christ's work. He does not limit himself to one single description but uses different ones to explain the work of Christ.

> You can say that Christ died for our sins. You may say that the Father has forgiven us because Christ has done for us what we ought to have done. You may say that we are washed in the blood of the Lamb. You may say that Christ defeated death. They are all true.[25]

CONCLUSION

Mere Christianity is the most direct, explicitly theological book of C. S. Lewis. While he has written other theological and apologetic works, none is as straightforward as this one. It is as close as he comes to writing what he would call real theology. He has brought with him his unique and refreshing perspective. Exploring this book, the reader begins to see that it is possible for any Christian to approach the mysteries of the faith. Not only the clergy and those with a formal theological education, but all Christians are able to think theologically. Lewis is not always successful. He oversteps his own self-imposed boundaries. He oversimplifies some complex teachings. But in the end, he presents the basic Christian teachings well, with lucidity and accuracy. Christ's identity and work are clearly proclaimed, explained, and defended. In these truths, we see God's answer to our world.

NOTES

1. 1. C. S. Lewis, *Mere Christianity* (New York: Macmillan, 1952), 6.
2. Ibid., 46, 47.
3. Ibid., 36.
4. Ibid., 39.
5. Ibid., 54.
6. Ibid.
7. Ibid., 55.
8. Ibid., 55–56.
9. Ibid., 56.
10. Ibid., 155.
11. Ibid.

12. Ibid., 164, 186, 158.
13. Ibid., 125.
14. Ibid., 142, 143.
15. Ibid., 143.
16. Ibid., 138.
17. Ibid., 150.
18. Ibid.
19. Ibid., 151.
20. Ibid., 152.
21. Ibid., 60.
22. Ibid., 57.
23. Ibid., 58.
24. Ibid., 61.
25. Ibid., 157.

Chapter Three

Miracles

A desire for a reasonable faith can lead people to question basic Christian teachings. We do not want to believe nonsense. We are afraid of being tricked or deceived. We want to see the proof for ourselves and are naturally skeptical of anything that is different from our own experience. Many people have questioned the reality of miracles and supernatural events. Can we accept parts of Christianity while leaving out miracles?

    C. S. Lewis was familiar with questions such as these because he had asked them himself. He also knew that removing supernatural elements would fatally undermine genuine Christianity. Because of this, Lewis addressed the historicity of miracles at various times during his career. He delivered sermons that addressed miracles, wrote letters to answer specific questions, and discussed miracles in many of his writings. His chief response is in his book *Miracles: A Preliminary Study*. As the title indicates, Lewis did not consider this book to be the final word on miracles. Indeed, he considered it to be merely the beginning of a conversation on the possibility and legitimacy of miracles. Because many objections to miracles are philosophical in nature, Lewis responds as a philosopher. He does not argue primarily from the biblical text but by means of logic. Nonetheless, portions of *Miracles* reveal Lewis's theological and Christological thought.

Natural and Supernatural

The key to understanding Lewis's discussion of miracles is the distinction between the views of naturalism and supernaturalism. Simply stated, a naturalist looks at the universe as a closed system. Nothing exists outside of nature. Conversely, a supernaturalist maintains that there is something beyond nature. Lewis cautions that this is not necessarily a discussion about the existence of God (or gods). Naturalists may believe in gods, but these will not be the same sort of gods found in a supernaturalist's worldview.

The distinction between these positions is crucial because it is one of presuppositions. A strictly naturalistic position entails a rejection of miracles. If miracles are always impossible, there will be no evidence sufficient to demonstrate their truth. A supernaturalist position, on the other hand, upholds the possibility of miracles. This does not assert the truth or historicity of any particular miracle but simply admits the possibility of miracles. The supernaturalist would still need to consider the evidence for any single event, but he would not categorically dismiss the possibility of miracles.

In the first edition of *Miracles*, Lewis uses human reason to argue that naturalism is self-defeating. He believed that thought itself was above nature because it can alter the natural world. Expanding on his work in *Mere Christianity*, Lewis considered the existence of ethical decisions and standards to be further evidence of the supernatural. In a truly closed system, there is no basis for evaluating right and wrong, yet we continually make ethical decisions. Lewis considered this to be further evidence that there is a supernatural domain. These arguments were quite controversial. After this conclusion was challenged, Lewis revised the book. Later editions do not say that naturalism is self-defeating, but Lewis still calls ethical decision-making the cardinal difficulty of naturalism.

What Are Miracles?

Lewis was a supernaturalist. He believed there was a possibility of things beyond our limited, natural world. In *Miracles*, he considers a few specific miracles but is more interested in the general possibility of miracles. But what is a miracle? It is vital that we understand Lewis's definition. A miracle is something that would not occur in the natural order of the universe. Lewis's definition does not go so far as to say that miracles are violations of natural law. Far from violating the laws of nature, miracles may be completely in accord with them. A miracle does, however, include something unexpected—a supernatural force. Because this divine power is the architect of the laws of nature, miracles are in conformity with the true natural laws.[1] Naturalists might view this as inconsistent, but they are missing data—supernatural data. Their system is consistent, but its boundaries are too small.

Lewis defends the possibility of miracles yet keeps them in limited parameters. Miracles may occur, and when they do, they are something different from what would ordinarily have happened, yet afterward the situation follows the normal laws of nature. So, for example, God might bring about a virgin birth by miraculously creating a sperm cell within a woman's womb. This creation is miraculous, but the resulting pregnancy is entirely ordinary and proceeds according to natural laws. Other miracles exhibit this same consistency. The miracle is followed by an existence in the natural order. God may miraculously create bread, or transform water into wine, yet when these things are consumed, they have the same effect as non-miraculous bread and wine.[2] Lewis's definition of *miracle* exists within carefully delineated bounds. Miraculous intervention may occur, but it does not continue as an ongoing state.

OBJECTIONS TO MIRACLES

As Lewis continues to define miracles, he deals with a number of objections, two of which are germane to this discussion. The first asserts the superiority of the modern mind over the primitive mind. This position claims that the people mentioned in the biblical accounts were too primitive to understand how nature works and so believed that something contrary to nature had occurred. Lewis cites the reaction of Joseph to the virgin birth. Joseph knew that a virgin conception was contrary to nature. It was not ignorance that caused his reaction to the angel's announcement, but faith and trust in God. Every objection we might raise to this miracle was known to Joseph. He could have rejected it; instead, he believed God. If he could believe this miracle, so can we.[3] The point is not that it was easy to believe the miracle but that it was equally difficult for Joseph to believe. Whether a culture is primitive or advanced does not discount the possibility of miracles.

The second objection involves the question of life on other planets. Lewis notes that the possibility of other life-forms in the universe is used in two contradictory arguments, both of which are marshaled against Christianity. On the one hand, if there is life on other worlds, this is used to argue against the truth of Christianity. If many planets support life, why should we be so presumptuous to believe that God would take a special interest in humanity? Why should He become incarnate to save human beings? On the other hand, if earth is unique in supporting life, it is argued that this life must be accidental. According to this argument, if God were truly the creator, He would have put life on many planets. Either situation is used to attempt to disprove Christianity.[4]

The question is not one of theology but one of simple logic. Neither option affects the truthfulness of Christianity. Because there is no clear revelation of other planetary life in the Christian faith, and because science has not, as yet, provided evidence one way or the other, the question remains open. Lewis summarizes the possibilities: It may be that the universe is filled with unfallen creatures that have never needed redemption. Perhaps it is full of beings who have been redeemed in the same manner we were. The universe may have other things of interest to God than life as we know it.[5] The point is, this question doesn't affect this discussion. Whether there is life on other planets has nothing to do with the possibility of miracles. It merely expands the question of their possibility. It is interesting, however, to note that Lewis considers this question in light of the redemption. Would other life-forms need salvation? Lewis does not address the question in detail here, but he does explore the question in a fictional context in his Space Trilogy. The question continued to interest Lewis, but, in the end, it remains unanswered.

THE NECESSITY OF MIRACLES FOR CHRISTIANITY

After concluding that miracles are possible, Lewis considers their necessity. Might they be removed to provide a simplified Christianity? Lewis believes that this simplification of Christianity is futile. It fails to understand what Christianity really is. Other religions might remain intact if miracles are removed. Lewis notes that you could remove miracles from Hinduism without changing any essential teachings. Removing miracles from Islam would have only a minor effect on the religion. This is not true of Christianity. The Christian faith is grounded in an incredible miracle. Christianity is destroyed when miraculous or supernatural elements are removed. They are what distinguish it from other religions.[6]

Lewis was interested in the teachings of other religions. He saw the necessity of miracles as a unique characteristic of Christianity. Christianity is precisely the story of a great miracle. That miracle is Jesus Christ and, in particular, His incarnation and redemptive work. Without these miracles, Christianity fades away.

ANTHROPOMORPHIC LANGUAGE

Lewis addresses one further obstacle that may impair understanding of miracles. The descriptive and anthropomorphic language employed by the Bible may be difficult for a modern person to accept as literally true. This language may seem hopelessly outdated. God is said to have a Son. How is this different than any of the mythological deities? This Son came down from heaven, descended into hell, and ascended again into heaven. Does this mean that heaven is located just up in the sky or in the clouds? Is hell found in the center of the earth? It may even seem to imply that the earth itself is flat. Looking at these, and other images, the modern reader might conclude that Christianity presupposes a view of the universe that has long since been discarded. How could rational adults return to such teachings?[7]

Anthropomorphic images are freely used in Scripture. Moreover, many Christians hold these images in the literal sense that Lewis describes. Yet genuine Christianity clearly maintains that the images are descriptive. For example, Christians might picture the Father as having a human body while simultaneously confessing that He has no body. They may envision the Father as older than the Son, but the Christian faith maintains that both exist eternally.[8] Scripture contains descriptive language, but it also explains and deepens the images. Most Christians realize that their mental images fall short of the reality. Lewis suggests that critics look only at a portion of what is really said. In particular, he cautions that one must not judge Christianity (or anything else) from the ideas of children. Images of childish imagination are not the substance of the Christian faith that is held by adults. Still, some adults conceive of these matters in primitive images. Explaining the significance of this, Lewis observes that it is difficult to communicate abstract subjects without using descriptive or anthropomorphic language. Some Christians have attempted to remove this type of language, but all they succeed in doing is replacing one image with another.[9] This is the essence of Lewis's understanding of images—they are necessary for understanding. If images are used, they might as well be familiar, concrete images that communicate rather than abstractions.

When images are used properly, they provide illustration and analogy of that which is difficult to understand. When examining the images of the New Testament, the reader should look not only at the image employed, but also at the full meaning of that image. Consider, for example, the New Testament's description of the Second Person of the Trinity as the Son. Some might describe this language as primitive or compare it to mythological deities. An honest evaluation of Scripture, however, will also reveal other descriptions of the Son. John 1 describes Him as the *Logos,* the eternal Word who was with God and was God. Colossians 1 describes Christ as the creator who holds the entire universe together. Ephesians 1 reveals that all things will reach their fulfillment in Him.[10] Far from presenting a primitive or naïve depiction of Christ, Lewis demonstrates that it uses highly sophisticated, precise language along with descriptive and evocative images.

Lewis continues to explain the images. Saying that God has a Son does not mean that He reproduces sexually. The word "Son" does not mean precisely the same thing when it is applied to the Trinity as it does when describing mere humans. This does not, however, give us license to change the clear meaning of Scripture. Events that our senses can experience and our language fully express are described as they literally occurred. For example, Scripture is not using this anthropomorphic language when it says that Jesus changed water into wine. Our words are able to communicate this event clearly.[11]

Images are helpful to explain difficult or abstract concepts. The relationship between the persons of the Trinity is a key example. Because this relationship is beyond any direct human experience, the only way it may be discussed is by analogy or metaphor. Such expressions are useful, but they ought not be pressed beyond their intended sense.

CHRISTOLOGICAL MIRACLES

THE INCARNATION

After dealing with fundamental objections to miracles and challenging the presuppositions of critics, Lewis begins to consider specific biblical miracles. When miracles are examined, readers often address their attention to things Jesus did for others. These are miracles, but Lewis considered them to be of secondary importance. The most significant and important miracles are the incarnation and resurrection. Of these two prime miracles, Lewis is most concerned with the incarnation, which he terms "the Grand Miracle." The biblical truth that God Himself has taken on a human nature lies at the heart of Christianity. All other miracles, and indeed all of Christianity, relate to this miracle. Secondary miracles prepare for Christ's incarnation, demonstrate its reality, or directly result from it. Truly there is nothing analogous to this miracle. Indeed, if it occurred, it is not only the heart of Christianity, it is the most important event in all of history.[12]

The challenge of this doctrine, of course, is that God becomes man. In this unparalleled miracle, God willingly becomes a part of His creation, taking on human limitations. This teaching is impossible to ignore. Echoing his argumentation from *Mere Christianity*, Lewis writes that we may not easily dispense with Jesus' claims to be God. It is illogical to consider Him to be simply a good teacher.

In *Mere Christianity*, Lewis suggested that there are only three logical answers to the question of Jesus' identity. He might have been a lunatic, a devil, or the Son of God. In *Miracles*, Lewis distills the possibilities to two. Either Jesus is God or He is profoundly insane. Once again, Lewis demonstrates the rational conclusion. One might argue that Jesus was insane, but the depth and the sanity of His teaching argues against this.[13] The only logical conclusion that remains is that Jesus is divine.

Assuming the deity of Christ does not, however, answer the questions of the incarnation. One might fully assert the deity of

Christ yet deny His humanity, thus embracing the ancient heresy of Docetism. Lewis, therefore, continues his examination of the incarnation in more detail. He explains the union of the two natures of Christ by reverting to his earlier discussion of reason. Reason is supernatural, according to Lewis's argument. If this is true, then a human being is a union of two distinct natures: natural and supernatural. Lewis uses this twofold nature to illustrate the incarnation.

How can God become man? How can a human nature and a divine nature, as different as they are, be united in one person? Lewis says that this would be a fatal stumbling block if we were not already familiar and comfortable with the dichotomy of nature and the supernatural within us. We ourselves have natural bodies, but we also have the ability to reason. If reason is, as Lewis argues, supernatural, we represent a similar type of union. As our bodies are united with the ability to reason, so Christ has a human nature united with His divine nature. This analogy has its limits, however. Lewis quickly qualifies that the supernatural element of an ordinary human being remains part of God's creation while in Christ it is the creator Himself who is united to a human nature.[14]

This argument is only as strong as the analogy. Lewis claims that the personal union would be a *fatal* stumbling block if we were not already familiar with the dichotomy of the natural and the supernatural within us. In this, he is incorrect. The dichotomous nature of an individual is not self-evident nor does the lack of this philosophical construct destroy the personal union of Christ. This example might be helpful as a possible explanation. The Athanasian Creed uses it as an illustration of the incarnation, but it is just that—an illustration. The truth of the incarnation is not dependent on the strength of this analogy. If he had sought other images to supplement his proposal, it might have worked. But to say that without this image the personal union would be a fatal stumbling block is a most regrettable error.

This passage may be significant for another reason as well because in it Lewis comes close to the Eutychian heresy. Eutychianism claims that the two natures of Christ were totally mingled together and indistinguishable. Lewis writes that we consist of our natural being united with the supernatural element of reason. In his example, natural self and reason may not be distinguished by many readers but may appear to be so unified that the self is perceived as a complete unity. If the human and divine natures of Christ are so united, the natures may be indistinct. Yet having used imprecise wording, Lewis qualifies his statements, saying, "I do not think anything we do will enable us to imagine the mode of consciousness of the incarnate God."[15]

After experimenting with new formulations, Lewis retreats to mystery. There is no doubt that Lewis believed the incarnation to be fact and was attempting to explain it in a way that would make sense to skeptics. Lewis was not a Eutychian. Unfortunately, he employed a suspect comparison and so has called his entire argument into question.

Lewis adds another facet to his examination of the incarnation when he looks at the conception of Christ. For Lewis, the challenge of the incarnation is the personal union of Christ. If that question is resolved, the virgin birth is much easier to accept. It is simply another miracle performed by the power of God. The Lord of all creation uses His life-creating power once more so a virgin can conceive.[16] After this conception the miracle is complete and a normal pregnancy proceeds apart from miraculous intervention. Once the event occurs, nature continues according to its normal patterns.

ILLUSTRATING THE INCARNATION

In philosophical argument, Lewis inadequately discusses the incarnation. By anchoring his argument to one particular philosophical construct, he sets himself up for defeat. As he continues his discussion of the incarnation, however, he returns to descriptive language and illustration. Lewis writes about the incarnation, vividly employing the motif of descent and ascent in three different ways.

In the first instance, Lewis describes the work of Christ in the incarnation by a direct discussion of God's work and the biological events through which the incarnation took place.

> God descends to re-ascend. He comes down; down from the heights of absolute being into time and space, down into humanity; down further still, if embryologists are right, to recapitulate in the womb ancient and pre-human phases of life; ... He goes down to come up again and bring the whole ruined world up with Him.[17]

Lewis is citing a developmental theory—ontogeny recapitu-lates philogeny—that was popular in his time but has since been abandoned. This theory posited that one can retrace evolutionary development in embryology. Hence, a developing fetus appears to display gills, a tail, or other features of lower animals. While embryologists no longer hold to this developmental theory, con-sider how Lewis uses this progression. He clearly maintains that the Christ was incarnate within the womb. His descent into humanity went even further than might be imagined—even lower in the evolutionary cycle. Christ humbled Himself to be the low-est of His creation. This passage might well be read in parallel with Lewis's controversial words from *Mere Christianity* that to under-stand the drastic change Christ undertook in the incarnation, one might have to imagine becoming a slug or a crab. Here Lewis takes the position that through embryology Christ did precisely that! He humbled Himself even beneath humanity, into the lowest state of His creation. But having descended, He comes up again and brings the whole world with Him. Lewis does not restrict the work of Christ to humanity. His work affects the entire world.

From this direct passage, Lewis moves immediately to two illustrations. The first is the image of a strongman who struggles to lift an enormous weight. He crouches beneath this object to raise it. The enormity of his task nearly overcomes him when, sud-denly, he stands. He lifts the object from the ground and carries it away.[18] Now the imaginative mind of Lewis is unleashed. This time the humiliation of Christ is described as a change not of physical state, but of place. To lift, the strongman must stoop, nearly disappearing under the load. The man's strength and his person are unaltered, but in stooping to accomplish his task, he almost disappears. This image involves no incarnation or change, but it is entirely focused on work. Thus, by itself, it is inadequate, but it nonetheless partially illustrates the humiliation of Christ. The act of the strongman, the raising of the burden, is described as incredible. So it is with the work of Christ. He lowers Himself, almost disappearing in death before rising from the dead. As Christ rises, He raises His creation to life again.

The third image is perhaps the most vivid. Lewis compares Christ to a man who strips himself of his clothing and dives into incredibly deep water to find a precious object. Near the surface, the warm water is still affected by the light of the sun, but the deeper he goes, the darker and colder the water becomes. The man descends to the depths of the water where nothing lives and where the lack of illumination obscures all color and distinction. The diver returns from this unfathomable depth, bringing with him the singular object he was seeking. Both the diver and his treasure now appear in their true color once more.[19]

Before beginning his heroic task, the diver stripped, setting aside his clothes. Similarly, Christ sets aside the regular use of His divine power and glory. The farther down the diver goes, the more his appearance changes. He descends to the very depths of death and decay, evoking Christ's descent into hell. Finally, the diver returns and reveals his precious prize. The image combines a treasure-seeking diver with birth imagery. After returning to the surface, both the diver and the object are restored to their natural state and visible for what they really are.

In each of these images, Lewis reveals his view of the incarnation. Individually, they are prone to greater error than when taken as a whole. The first passage, dealing with embryology, presents the union of Christ's two natures but falls short because of the outdated and controversial scientific explanation. The image of the strongman notes the work of Christ, but it lacks any incarnation imagery. The third passage seems to imply a change in the diver who lost his color, but as he emerges from the water, he is essentially unchanged. Taken together, however, the images are balanced. Together, they show the extreme change of the incarnation, the extent of the humiliation, and Christ's desire to raise and ennoble His people.

THE CORN KING

Lewis has employed three depictions of descent and reascent. After doing so, he reminds his readers that this image is known in many cultures all over the world. The incarnation of Christ is the highest expression of a pattern seen in nature and in mythology.[20] In presenting this next image, he again considers a myth of near-universal scope, that of the "Corn King." This myth depicts a harvest deity who annually dies and comes to life again. Many cultures have versions of this myth. Lewis does not believe that Christianity appropriated this story; instead, Christ is the archetype. In fact, Christianity differs significantly from Corn King mythology by failing to fit predictably into the pattern. To a certain degree, Christ is like the mythological harvest deities. Similar to Adonis or Osiris, Jesus is said to be divine and dies to rise again. Unlike these gods, or any of the other mythological gods, however, Jesus Christ was a historical person. Lewis specifically notes that we don't know where, when, or even if these other figures actually lived. In contrast, the gospels are remarkably specific regarding the historical details of our Savior's life.

Like these mythological gods, Christ dies and rises again. He enacts this mythology but does not use it in His teaching. Lewis finds this the most peculiar thing about Christianity. Of all the figures who embody the pattern of the dying and living God, only Jesus Christ is historical. Yet even when He enacts the essential features of these myths, He makes no explicit connection to them. Most surprising to Lewis is that Jesus even takes bread and says that it is His body. We might expect that He would specifically connect to these myths in the Sacrament, but He does not.[21] There is no trace of these nature religions in Christ's teaching. He fulfills and exceeds these religions by being the only historical person to enact them. He truly dies and rises again, yet makes no appeal to the natural cycle or to the nature religions. This argument is essential to Lewis. He embraces the truthful elements of the world's myths but knows their limits. Where there is a divergence, Lewis follows Christianity.

Without a doubt, the greatest divergence is seen in the identity of the divine figure: Christians do not claim that Jesus is a god or one of the gods. Rather, in the incarnation, the one true God, who identified Himself to the Jews as Yahweh, has come into His creation. He is incarnate, dies, and rises again. This work is done once for all humanity. In the great myths, the god is tied to nature, dying and rising each year. The true God does not do this. He is not part of nature, but He is nature's creator. The truth is that "He is not a nature-God, but the God of Nature. ... He is like the Corn-King because the Corn-King is a portrait of Him."[22]

The incarnation does not involve a nebulous deity. Christ is clearly identified with Yahweh, the Creator. He does not derive from nature; He is God. Lewis believes that the world is filled with images of the Corn King and other myths of the dying God because they are patterned on the real occurrence of the incarnation. Christ is God incarnate, a theme that has been restated many times throughout nature, but Christ is the archetype.

THE WORK OF CHRIST

To call the incarnate Christ the archetype of the Corn King and the dying god myths describes a great deal of His person and work, but it is an incomplete description. The work of Christ is far above that which is depicted in mythology. Lewis discusses the specifics of the person and work of Christ in the chapter "The Grand Miracle" and in the following chapters, where a more developed presentation of Christology emerges.

Christ is uniquely incarnate. While Lewis seems receptive to diverse speculation on open questions of Scripture, he is remarkably focused here. He considers the possibility that there may be other creatures in the universe who need redemption. As he speculates about this, he expresses his doubt that the Son of God has repeatedly become incarnate for each type of fallen creature. Rather, if there are other creatures in need of redemption, they will be redeemed in some other fashion. The incarnation of Jesus Christ is a singular event.[23] Typically, Lewis speculates but does not impose his conclusions on others. Indeed, here he does not even offer a conclusion. He simply states, on aesthetic grounds, that the incarnation must be unique.

After coming to earth, Christ continues His work. That work, of course, includes miracles. One might suppose that a book about miracles would contain a great emphasis on the miracles of Jesus Christ. Surprisingly, Lewis notes only a few specific miracles performed by Christ. Significant are miracles connected with the understanding of Christ as the archetypal Corn King, including the feeding of the five thousand. In discussing these miracles, Lewis again hesitates to draw conclusions. Precisely how is it that Christ is able to perform miracles? Were these acts only made possible by His deity, or was He able to do these things because He was a perfect man? While these questions have intriguing ramifications, Lewis is not overly concerned. Without defining the mechanism that made them possible, Lewis is content to state that Christ did the miracles.[24]

As discussion of Christ's work continues, Lewis notes that it is focused on suffering. Echoing the words of Isaiah, he describes the Messiah as a man of sorrows. Although He is God and worthy of honor and worship, He is most notable for His suffering.[25] It is not merely suffering but sacrifice and death that characterize His work. He is the fatted calf that is killed for the prodigal son. He is the eternal Lamb, slain to take away the sins of the world. Indeed, as Revelation 13:8 indicates, this Lamb was slain before the creation of the work to save His people.[26] That sacrifice, in its full effect and with all its ramifications, is beyond our ability to apprehend, but it is joyfully believed. The work of Christ is intrinsically connected to suffering and death—a death that we deserved.

If humanity is to be saved, it must be through the death of one who voluntarily chooses his fate. No ordinary human can do. A perfect human must die the perfect death. Only the incarnate God has the necessary perfection. He dies in the place of every other person. Lewis says that the victory Christ has accomplished can be described either as the defeat of death or its redemption.[27] Lewis is, in essence, providing an exposition of the Anselmic theory of the atonement, a theory that he repeatedly claims to find difficult. Yet true to his other writings on atonement, he presents himself as holding no particular theory. It makes no difference whether you say that Christ has defeated death or whether you describe His victory as the redemption of death.

THE RESURRECTION

Following Christ's vicarious death is the uniqueness of the resurrection. This is different from other miracles of the Bible, different from things that are claimed to be miraculous today, even different from other biblical resurrections. In a key passage, Lewis declares the resurrection to be a pivotal event. Never before had something like this happened. Echoing Paul's words in 1 Corinthians 15 that call Christ the "firstfruits of those who have fallen asleep," Lewis calls Him the firstfruits and describes his victory: "He has forced open a door that has been locked since the death of the first man. He has met, fought, and beaten the King of Death."[28] Here the work of Christ is seen as a battle. The imagery is clearly that of *Christus Victor*—another theory of the atonement. Lewis has chosen diverse elements of two separate atonement theories and employs both as he sees fit.

CONCLUSION

In *Miracles*, Lewis had mixed success in dealing with objections to the idea of miracles. Often the effectiveness of his arguments wanes because it is based on his own questions, not all of which are shared by skeptics. He frequently limits his arguments to narrow points that may not concern other people. The work is far from exhaustive in approaching the many miraculous narratives of the Scriptures. Yet by its very structure, it makes a critical point: The chief miracles are those surrounding the person and work of Christ. These are not miracles done to demonstrate His identity, but miracles involving His very nature. It simply must be this way. The incarnation and resurrection are grand miracles around which revolves the Christian faith. Ultimately, they must be the focus.

NOTES

1. C. S. Lewis, *Miracles* (New York: Macmillan, 1947), 44, 58.
2. Ibid., 59–60.
3. Ibid., 48.
4. Ibid., 50.
5. Ibid., 51–52.
6. Ibid., 68.
7. Ibid., 68–69.
8. Ibid., 73.
9. Ibid., 74.
10. Ibid., 76.
11. Ibid., 80.
12. Ibid., 108.
13. Ibid., 109.
14. Ibid., 110.
15. Ibid.
16. Ibid., 139.
17. Ibid., 111.
18. Ibid.
19. Ibid., 111–12.
20. Ibid., 112.
21. Ibid., 113–14.
22. Ibid., 114–15.
23. Ibid., 124.
24. Ibid., 135.
25. Ibid., 118.
26. Ibid., 122, 125.
27. Ibid., 130.
28. Ibid., 145.

Chapter Four

Introduction
to the Fictional Writings

Reading through the Christian works of C. S. Lewis, it is easy to forget that he was not a theologian. Lewis was a professor of literature who wrote a number of theological works. Yet as he frequently reminds his readers, he was a layman and an amateur in theology. In his fictional works, however, Lewis leaves his amateur status behind for the strengths of his academic discipline. He uses his literary talents to create a variety of fictional writings. While these writings are not overtly theological or apologetic, they do contain significant Christian content. Understanding the nature of these writings will help us understand the theological or apologetic content as well.

THE NEED FOR METAPHORIC LANGUAGE

C. S. Lewis believed that metaphors and descriptive language are necessary for human communication. We may think that we describe things literally, but very little language is absolutely literal. In fact, many words that are thought to be literal are really metaphors whose metaphorical meaning has been forgotten over time. Whether we know it or not, we often use metaphorical language, and our understanding is often directly connected to these metaphors.

Lewis applies this in his apologetic works when he considers anthropomorphic language. Language that describes God in human terms has its limitations, but would its removal improve our understanding? In his essay "Horrid Red Things," Lewis considers the possibility of replacing anthropomorphic language in the creed with philosophic language. He readily acknowledges that the creeds, like the Scriptures behind them, use metaphorical description. To say that the Son of God first "came down" and later "ascended into heaven," as the Nicene Creed proclaims, is to use spatial imagery. Taken in a literal, spatial, sense, these words could lead to the conclusion that heaven is physically located above the clouds. Is there a better, more literal, way to describe this? Could we depict Christ's coming in terms of entering the physical universe from a spiritual dimension? Might it be described with the categories of the noumenal and phenomenal or some other philosophical construct? Lewis considers these alternatives only to conclude that these new descriptions are just as metaphorical as the phrases they are designed to replace. Nearly all human language is inextricably bound to metaphor. Replacing the traditional, creedal language will not excise metaphor; we will only succeed in replacing the metaphorical images with new metaphors. We may even find ourselves in a worse situation by replacing a known metaphor with another unrecognized metaphor. All too frequently, the substitute metaphor lacks the richness of the image that it replaced. Lewis summarizes this conundrum, saying, "we can make our language more polysyllabic and duller: we cannot make it more literal."[1]

The idea is reiterated in "Is Theology Poetry?" in which Lewis notes that Christianity cannot restate its beliefs apart from metaphor and symbol.[2] The images and metaphors are necessary if we are to communicate. Lewis embraces this idea throughout his writings, but he does so deliberately in his fictional works. His theology is expressed through metaphor and other poetic language.

ALLEGORY

To say that Lewis deliberately uses metaphor, however, does not define the genre of his fiction. Does he use poetic language to such an extent that his works become allegorical? The answer depends on the definition of allegory. If by allegory one means that a narrative has secondary or parallel meanings, then much, if not all, of Lewis's fiction is clearly allegorical. But this imprecise definition is not one that Lewis used. He defines allegory as a composition that uses physical objects or characters to represent immaterial things. For example, erotic love might be pictured by Cupid. This love is an experience, but it is represented by something more tangible.[3] He clarifies this idea in his masterwork, *The Allegory of Love*:

> [Y]ou can start with immaterial fact, such as the passions which you actually experience, and can then invent *visibilia* to express them. If you are hesitating between an angry retort and a soft answer, you can express your state of mind by inventing a person called *Ira* with a torch and letting her contend with another invented person called *Patientia*. This is allegory.[4]

Allegory is not merely a story with an additional meaning, or even a story with a fixed second meaning. Rather, a work is allegorical when it presents characters or events specifically to express immaterial ideas, emotions, or identities. Lewis's prime example of allegory is John Bunyan's *The Pilgrim's Progress*. In this classic allegory, the protagonist, "Christian," encounters a variety of obstacles on a journey. Lewis notes that, in one instance, Christian is held captive by "Giant Despair." This is allegorical because despair is an immaterial emotion personified by Bunyan. The Giant imprisons Christian, even as despair can cause a person to feel imprisoned.[5]

If one accepts Lewis's focused definition of allegory, it becomes apparent that none of the books considered in this section are truly allegorical. While all have deeper meanings, these meanings are not visible presentations of invisible things.

SYMBOLIC AND SACRAMENTAL WRITING

If Lewis's fiction is not allegorical, the question of genre remains. How should these books be described? In *The Allegory of Love*, after narrowly defining allegory, Lewis delineates another possibility.

> But there is another way of using the equivalence, which is almost the opposite of allegory, and which I would call sacramentalism or symbolism. If our passions, being

immaterial, can be copied by material inventions, then it is possible that our material world in its turn is a copy of an invisible world. ... The attempt to read that something else through its sensible imitations, to see that archtype in the copy, is what I mean by symbolism or sacramentalism. ... The difference between the two can hardly be exaggerated. The allegorist leaves the given—his own passions—to talk about that which is confessedly less real. The symbolist leaves the given to find that which is more real. To put the difference in another way, for the symbolist it is we who are the allegory. We are the "frigid personifications." The world which we mistake for reality is the flat outline of that which elsewhere veritably is in all the round of its unimaginable dimensions.[6]

This understanding, first outlined by Plato, attempts to reveal the highest reality through the things of this world. Both the allegorist and the symbolist look outside of this world but in opposite directions. The allegorist looks to internal emotions and becomes subjective, while the symbolist looks outward for objectivity. So Lewis claims that he is not attempting to reflect his own thought and emotion, rather he seeks to reveal archetypal truths.

SUPPOSAL

Lewis expresses similar ideas when he describes his writings as "supposals." This description frees him from the necessity of following any other story precisely, including the Gospels, while allowing him to use elements as he desires. So, for example, when asked if the Narnian stories were allegorical, Lewis responded:

If Aslan represented the immaterial deity, he would be an allegorical figure. In reality, however, he is an invention giving an imaginary answer to the question, "What might Christ have become like if there really were a world like Narnia and He chose to be incarnate and die and rise again in *that* world as He actually has done in ours?" This is not allegory at all.[7]

He goes on to say that *Perelandra* is, likewise, a supposition. In this case, he imagines another planet where another couple faces temptation. Unlike the earthly story, this couple does not fall into sin. Calling his writing "supposals" allows Lewis to use elements from other sources creatively without worrying about changing facts or speculating on details.

MYTH

Lewis also described his fictional works as myths. In *An Experiment in Criticism*, he defines myth, saying that a true myth has six characteristics. First, while the myth is reflected in a story, it is not restricted to any one story. It will inevitably have expressions in other narratives and forms. Each retelling may have different details, but the basic myth will be present in various accounts. Second, a true myth is not reliant on suspense or surprise to engage the reader. In fact, Lewis says, the plot of a genuine myth will likely seem inevitable. Despite knowing how the story will end, the myth can continue to engage and captivate the reader. Because of this, a myth can be unoriginal yet still be a wonderful example of a myth. Third, myth generally makes few appeals to sympathy. The reader may not share the emotion of the characters yet may enjoy reading the myth. Fourth, a genuine myth will contain some impossible, supernatural, or fantastic element. Fifth, myth is not comic but serious. It may fill the reader with sadness or joy but not in a flippant manner. Finally, a myth is recognized by the response that it engenders in the reader. It may fill the reader with awe, longing, or expectation.[8]

The challenge of such a multifaceted definition of myth, and consequently of Lewis's application of it in his fiction, is that the mythical character is dependent more upon the response of the reader than on the text itself. Accordingly, one reader may find a story mythical, while another reader does not.[9] One reader may find a deeper meaning in the book, while another may see nothing but the literal meaning, yet both readers have read appropriately. Lewis would neither stifle the reader who found depth in the book nor demand that all readers discover that depth. It is this flexibility that shows the difference between allegory and other forms of poetic language. A reader who does not understand the allegorical meaning does not understand the book. But if a work is symbolical or mythical, readers will be rewarded with the story itself, regardless of whether they find other meanings.

Lewis emphatically denied that his works were allegorical, yet by means of imaginative language, he constructed creative narratives filled with meaning beyond their face value. These second meanings are not to be forced on the reader, but the reader who sees them will find great depth in Lewis's fiction.

NOTES

1. C. S. Lewis, "Horrid Red Things," in *God in the Dock: Essays on Theology and Ethics*, ed. Walter Hooper (Grand Rapids: Eerdmans, 1970), 71.

2. C. S. Lewis, "Is Theology Poetry?" in *The Weight of Glory and Other Addresses* (New York: Macmillan, 1980), 87.

3. Letter to a lady, 29 December 1958, in *The Letters of C. S. Lewis,* ed. W. H. Lewis (New York: Harcourt, Brace, Jovanovich, 1966), 283.

4. C. S. Lewis, *The Allegory of Love: A Study in Medieval Tradition* (London: Oxford University Press, 1936), 44.

5. Letter to a lady, 29 December 1958, in *Letters of C. S. Lewis*, 283.

6. Lewis, *Allegory of Love*, 44, 45.

7. Letter to a lady, 29 December 1958, in *Letters of C. S. Lewis*, 283.

8. C. S. Lewis, *An Experiment in Criticism* (Cambridge: Cambridge University Press, 1961), 43–44.

9. Lewis, *Experiment in Criticism*, 45.

Chapter Five

The Space Trilogy

C. S. Lewis loved books that could transport the reader into unimagined situations or other worlds. From ancient myths to modern fiction, he appreciated stories that surprised, challenged, and delighted the reader. He was particularly intrigued by the ability of science fiction to present richly creative scenes. It is not surprising, then, that his first novels were in this genre.

The three books in the Space Trilogy tell the story of Professor Elwin Ransom, a professor of philology at Cambridge University. Through all three books, Lewis creates a unique blend of early science fiction, fantasy, and Christian myth.

In *Out of the Silent Planet*, Ransom is kidnapped by two evil men who take him to the planet Malacandra (Mars). They intend to offer him as a sacrifice to the inhabitants of the planet. When Ransom escapes, he meets the creatures of that planet and discovers that it is an unfallen world. The creatures teach him the "Old Solar" language and instruct him about God, whom they call Maleldil. In the end, all the humans are sent back to Earth.

In the second novel, *Perelandra*, Ransom is transported to the planet Perelandra (Venus). Weston, one of the men who originally kidnapped him, also arrives on that planet, though now he is demon-possessed. Perelandra is a newly created world, and Weston tries to tempt the first woman of that planet to fall into sin. After the woman resists his temptation, Ransom destroys

Weston, thus stopping temptation and preserving this perfect world.

The third novel, *That Hideous Strength*, brings the battle to Earth (Thulcandra). Ransom helps lead a group of faithful Christians who battle against evil men filled with satanic schemes.

Published between 1938 and 1945, these books show their age. They were written in an era when the nature and knowledge of science were different from today, and Lewis was no scientist. The contemporary reader may be amused at the conception of spacecraft or of descriptions of life on Mars and Venus. Yet there is an enduring charm to these books. The events are clearly fictional, but the narratives and the ideas underlying them are significant.

The Space Trilogy also has a notable theological dimension, but assessing this theology proves challenging. These books are first and foremost works of fiction. At the same time, Lewis deliberately uses deep mythological elements, writing simultaneously on multiple levels. While these layers of understanding should not be forced on the reader, they are present and help reveal more of Lewis's theology.

MALELDIL

Filling the three novels is the divine character, Maleldil. Lewis clearly portrays this character, revealing him through his work, through the response of his creatures, and ultimately, by equating him with Jesus Christ. This identification begins with his name. Lewis uses his linguistic talents throughout these books as he creates the Old Solar language. Consider some of the words Lewis invents:

Handra—earth, the ground
Malacandra—the planet Mars, the planet as a whole
Eldil—"angel," intelligence
Maleldil—God

Prefixes and suffixes expand root words. Hence the word *handra*, the element earth or dirt, can be modified. Altered to *Harandra*, it means mountains or high earth. Prefixed with *Thulc*, it means silent planet or the Earth. Prefixed with *Mala*, it is the name of the planet Mars, *Malacandra*. This prefix appears to be derived from the Greek adverb *mala*, which means "very" or "exceedingly." Thus, *Malacandra* might be rendered "the greater land, the whole of the earth," or simply "the planet." Expanding the language further, an *eldil* is a noncorporeal life-form, similar to an angel. The greatest of the *eldila* that are encountered are the *Oyeresu*. But greater than these and all other beings is *Maleldil*, one who is *Mal-eldil*, greater than the *eldila*, the greatest spiritual being.

THE PERSON AND WORK OF MALELDIL

CREATION

Philology may provide an understanding of what Lewis was attempting, but it is the contextual reading of his work that must be definitive. Who is Maleldil, and what does he do? First, Maleldil is the creator. This emerges as Ransom learns about Malacandra. When he learns that the planet is ruled by Oyarsa, he asks if Oyarsa was the creator. The hrossa are shocked that this adult lacks the knowledge of a child: that the world was created and is ruled by Maleldil the Young.[1] While Maleldil made Malacandra, on Perelandra (Venus), the specifics of creation are carried out on his behalf by the Oyarsa of Perelandra. Nevertheless, Maleldil remains the creator, making the beings who occupy the worlds.

Maleldil's work on Earth is revealed more explicitly in *That Hideous Strength*. In this book, Jane listens as Ransom and his associates describe Christianity not as a "religion" nor with mystical depictions, but in terms of the strong, purposeful work of God who is actively involved in His creation. During this conversation, the names of God and Maleldil are used for the same being.[2]

In creation, all hnau (including humans) are made in the image of Maleldil. Although the Oyeresu do not have corporeal bodies, both Ransom and the Oyarsa are "copies of Maleldil." Likewise, the king and queen of Perelandra arc "images of Maleldil," who is the creator of the universe and of life.

PROVIDENCE

Following creation, Maleldil remains active in his creation. His providence is seen in the procreation of the hrossa on Malacandra, who have few offspring despite the pleasure of begetting them. When asked why they do not have more offspring, they simply answer that this is the way that Maleldil made them. Maleldil's providence is also mediated through the Oyeresu.

When the great war of heaven took place, the "bent" Oyarsa of Thulcandra (Satan) was defeated and driven back to his own planet. There, following Maleldil's directions, the Oyeresu and eldila bound the bent Oyarsa to the air so he could not leave that world.[3]

Because Satan had damaged Malacandra, Maleldil guided Malacandra's Oyarsa in reforming the planet so life could survive. Maleldil's influence extends to Earth as well. He charges Ransom with watching over the evil men Weston and Devine. Ransom is told that some eldila will help him and that Maleldil will show him what to do. Ransom was kidnapped to be brought to Mars, yet even this was within the plan of Maleldil, who caused it to happen for his own good purposes.

Maleldil's divinity is seen in the events surrounding death. One creature living on Malacandra says that death is the best drink of all because once he has tasted it, he will go to Maleldil. Similarly, when Ransom explains death to the lady of Perelandra, he says that when a person dies, Maleldil takes the soul out of the body and puts it somewhere else. It is hoped the soul is put in Deep Heaven. Maleldil's care extends through death.[4]

REDEMPTION

The supreme revelation of Maleldil's identity is seen in his redemption. Because there was no fall into sin on either Malacandra or Perelandra, the great act of divine redemption took place only once, on Earth. However, the specific details of Christ's work are not known on other planets. The Oyarsa of Malacandra suspects that something took place on Earth. He indicates that the Oyeresu suspected that Maleldil did not relinquish control of Earth to the bent Oyarsa. He alludes to stories told among the Oyeresu that Maleldil has done strange things to battle the bent Oyarsa on Earth. Still, he is ignorant about the details of the redemption, and has to seek knowledge of the actual events from Ransom. After Ransom explains, the Oyarsa marvels that Ransom has revealed wonders unknown in heaven. From this point on, the Oyeresu and eldila know exactly what took place. They have learned of the passion of Christ.[5]

More of the atonement is revealed as Ransom battles with demonic forces on Perelandra. The tempter tries to convince a woman to sin, claiming that the fall into sin was fortunate because it led to the goodness of the incarnation. Ransom answers that nothing can stop God's plan. His creatures cannot change His will. No matter what we do, God can make good come out of it. The conclusion will be good, but will it be the good that God had originally planned for us? How can we know what God would have done if we had not fallen into sin? Rather than debate this hypothetical situation, Ransom instead turns the attention back on the tempter, asking if he rejoices in the incarnation.[6]

Maleldil redeemed sinners by becoming man. This fact is abhorrent to the demons that possess Weston. Here, *Perelandra* interweaves two redemptive themes. Ransom realizes that he was brought to Perelandra to prevent another fall into sin. As he is trying to understand his own role, the Divine Voice surprises him by saying, "My name also is Ransom." As Ransom ponders these words, he suddenly sees the truth. God was not simply telling him about names; rather, He was communicating His office: "Maleldil, was the world's ransom. ..." This connection assures and strengthens Ransom, who realizes God was in control. "If he now failed, this world also would hereafter be redeemed. If he were not the ransom, another would be. ..."[7] Maleldil is Christ, who would be the ransom if Elwin Ransom failed to prevent the fall into sin. If necessary, God would redeem another world.

One more reflection of the atonement is found at the end of *Perelandra*. As the king of Perelandra cleans Ransom's injured foot, he comments on the blood that he sees flowing from the wound. Because he lives on an unfallen world that does not know the effects of sin, he has never seen blood before. Yet he knows what it is and notes its significance, saying, "[T]his is the substance wherewith Maleldil remade the worlds before any world was made."[8] With his blood, Maleldil remade the worlds. By this act of singular importance, all was transformed forever.

MALELDIL AND THE TRINITY

Not only is Maleldil the redeemer, but he also displays a complexity similar to the Holy Trinity. This initially appears through references to both Maleldil and Maleldil the Young. Ransom learns that there is only one God. That God is identified as Maleldil the Young.[9] Because Ransom does not yet understand, he asks where Maleldil lives. The hrossa respond that he lives with a being that they call "the Old One." Ransom asks about this "Old One" but cannot understand the answer. He only learns that he is incorporeal and doesn't live in any specific place.[10] The hrossa alone refer to the "Old One." This idea remains undeveloped until the second book, where the king of Perelandra provides more information. While the queen was being tempted, the king was learning more about Maleldil, Maleldil's Father, and "the Third One." There appears to be no direct contact with the Father (the hrossa's "Old One") and little revelation of his person or work. Even before the world was created, he knew the number of the elect and when the world would end.

Paralleling these passages are references to the Trinity. In the caves of Perelandra, Ransom crushes the head of the Un-man with the words of the trinitarian invocation. Likewise, when Ransom confronts Merlin, he commands him in Latin to identify himself, using the invocation.[11]

Here, as in the rest of Lewis's fiction, trinitarian statements are focused almost entirely on the Second Person. The Son creates, redeems, restores, and is the mediator between humanity and the rest of the Godhead. The precise roles of the Father and the Spirit concerning humanity are difficult to ascertain. If the other two persons are directly active, they are perceived as the Second Person of the Trinity. This is especially true of the Spirit. If a person knows Christ, he also knows the Father and the Spirit. Lewis lacks precision in his descriptions of Maleldil, but his intent is clearly to portray the Second Person of the Trinity and, through Him, to reveal the entire Godhead.

ATTRIBUTES OF MALELDIL

A good deal more may be known about Maleldil through his essential attributes, many of which are revealed while Ransom lives on Malacandra with the hrossa. Initially, Ransom considered it his responsibility to evangelize the creatures of Malacandra. He abandoned this idea when they began to catechize him. As his education progressed, the hrossa taught him that Maleldil does not have a physical body and is not subject to creaturely emotions or desires.[12]

Furthermore, Maleldil is omniscient, uniquely seeing everything. He alone sees his creatures as they really are.[13] Maleldil is also omnipresent. A litany of praise at the conclusion of *Perelandra* proclaims that all creation comes from Maleldil and he is the center of all things. He is present everywhere, not only part of him but his entire self. There is no limit to the divine presence. On the contrary, Maleldil is everywhere, even in the smallest imaginable places.[14] Furthermore, these words show that Maleldil worthily receives worship from his creatures. This fact is demonstrated again in *That Hideous Strength* when Ransom and Merlin join with the Oyeresu in worshiping Maleldil.

MALELDIL IS THE OBJECT OF FAITH

Finally, Maleldil is the object of faith. He is believed and trusted for salvation. On the unfallen worlds of Malacandra and Perelandra, all creatures believe. This is not the case on Earth. In *That Hideous Strength*, Ransom will not let the skeptical MacPhee search for Merlin because MacPhee has not placed himself under Maleldil's protection. A man who is sent to find Merlin is commended to his faith and encouraged to pray. Whatever happens, he will be safe in Maleldil's care.[15]

Lewis suggests one unusual aspect of faith, which is illustrated by Jane Studdock, who, in her youth, had rejected Christianity. Ransom asks if she is willing to pledge her obedience to Maleldil. Because Jane does not know Maleldil, she vows that she will obey Ransom. Surprisingly, he accepts this compromise. It is sufficient for that particular time but will not always be enough. Eventually, Maleldil will require her full obedience and love.[16]

This faith is such that Lewis says that the whole house—even the skeptical MacPhee—believed through the Director.[17] Such faith can be saving faith, but not indefinitely. The person eventually will need a proper, personal faith.

EXPLICIT IDENTIFICATION OF MALELDIL WITH GOD

Embedded within the Space Trilogy are a number of references that directly identify Maleldil. In *Perelandra*, the narrator walks toward Ransom's house and is tempted to turn back. He continues when he thinks of Maleldil, noting that Ransom identified Maleldil with God.[18] More explicitly, when Ransom is explaining the sorrow of death to the Lady of Perelandra, he alludes to the biblical story of Christ at the tomb of Lazarus, noting that even Maleldil wept when he saw death.[19]

There are also those occasions where Christian terminology is used, such as the uses of the invocation, which have been mentioned previously. When messengers are sent to find Merlin, the servants of Maleldil are to say that they have come in the name of God, the angels, and the powers of the planets.[20] Finally, when the time comes for Ransom to leave the Earth, he bids farewell to his friends: "Urendi Maleldil."[21] Although this phrase is untranslated, it is clearly a benediction. The name of Maleldil is used in blessing, as is the name of God.

THE INCARNATION

There is one further aspect of Maleldil that must be discussed: the incarnation and its impact on the universe. The incarnation affects the nature of intelligent life for all time. When Ransom meets the Lady of Perelandra, he is confused at her humanoid appearance. When he first traveled from Earth, he went to Malacandra where he encountered three types of sentient creatures. All three had different appearances, and none of them looked like humans. How was it that this woman shared human characteristics? The woman answered that sentient life appeared in these diverse forms only on worlds that were older than the Earth. When Ransom fails to understand, she explains that the incarnation has caused this change.[22] The incarnation has transformed reality. Intelligent life can henceforth be seen in no other form.

The incarnation is, furthermore, a source of comfort. Ivy Maggs confesses a fear of eldila, then remarks that she doesn't feel that way about God, though she knows that He should seem more frightening. Ransom explains that God was once terrifying to human beings, and angelic beings may continue to alarm mortals. "Angels in general are not good company for men in general. ... But as for Maleldil Himself, all that has changed by what happened at Bethlehem."[23]

The incarnation was an event of pivotal importance that altered the universe for all eternity. Reason can no longer be seen in another form, and now God is revealed and accessible through Jesus Christ. Taken as a whole, there is no doubt as to the identity of Maleldil. Lewis's presentation is highly centered on Christ. If his depiction of the Trinity is imprecise, it is, nevertheless, Christocentric. Key to Maleldil is the incarnation and redemption of the world. These are significant theological topics within a work of science fiction, but this is not the only Christological material. Lewis presents a second level of Christology in Elwin Ransom.

ELWIN RANSOM

OUT OF THE SILENT PLANET

Elwin Ransom emerges as a Christ figure as the Space Trilogy progresses. In the first book, *Out of the Silent Planet*, this aspect of his character is not fully developed. What is shown helps prepare the reader for Ransom's development in other books. Ransom, a professor of philology from Cambridge, is kidnapped and taken to Malacandra in place of another person. This substitution is the first time Elwin Ransom helps deliver another person, and it foreshadows his continuing work. When Ransom arrives on the new planet, he learns the language of the hnau there. Ransom teaches Oyarsa about the incarnation and atonement. At the end of the novel, he volunteers to return to Earth with Weston and Devine and to watch them. While these are significant acts, Ransom is not a developed Christ figure in this novel.

PERELANDRA

If *Out of the Silent Planet* is a preparatory narrative, *Perelandra* is a myth come of age. It recasts Genesis, revealing the struggle of all Christians against evil. Here Ransom clearly emerges as a Christ figure. He does not replace Jesus Christ, but he embodies and carries out Christlike work through each step of the narrative.

In the first book, Ransom was taken to Malacandra by force. In his second trip from Earth, the Oyarsa of Malacandra carries him to Perelandra in a coffinlike vessel. This vessel dissolves as it plunges into the sea, evoking images of birth and the watery rebirth of Baptism.[24] Through miraculous means, a man has been "born" on this planet for its salvation, yet Ransom does not know the reason for his presence. After his first night's sleep, he awakes in an edenic garden. Later, he meets the singular female inhabitant of Perelandra, a woman with green skin. When Ransom asks about her parents, she replies that she is *the* mother and her husband is *the* father on this planet. She responds to this truth in words of praise to Maleldil. Paralleling Mary's song, the Magnificat, she glorifies Maleldil for the incarnation and for his goodness to all creatures.[25]

It becomes more and more apparent as time goes on that Ransom is present in this perfect world to prevent its fall and put an end to temptation. The temptation comes through Ransom's one-time captor, Weston, who traveled to this planet in a spaceship. Eventually, Ransom sees that Weston is demon-possessed. After an extended verbal battle with Weston (now called "the Unman"), Ransom realizes that Maleldil has sent Ransom to be his representative. He knew that everything was in Maleldil's hands, but he came to realize that he and the lady were those hands. They were the embodiment of Maleldil's plan of deliverance. He gradually sees that his struggle will not be merely spiritual, but also physical. Temptation has been resisted, and the devil is not to be allowed to tempt forever. Yet if the temptation were to be stopped, it would only be stopped by Ransom.[26]

Ransom prepares to fight in the woman's stead, though he doubts his ability to succeed. A divine voice reassures him, telling him the significance of his name. Just as Christ came to earth to be a ransom, so this man was brought to Perelandra as a ransom.[27] Strengthened by the divine reassurance, Ransom resolves to fight the tempter, realizing that he is God's representative and that he has been divinely appointed to be a substitutionary ransom. But Maleldil remained in control of his creation. If Ransom did not succeed, then Maleldil would undoubtedly have another plan. He was on Perelandra as Maleldil's representative, yet this is not an unusual situation. Many people are called to be God's representatives. Every time an individual takes a stand for God or does a good work according to God's will, he or she represents Him.[28]

Lewis is intertwining parallel Christ figures. Ransom stands for Maleldil no more, and no less, than others who resist the devil or do good works. Fighting for Maleldil is simply an application of his faith. Ransom does this without concern for himself, though he realizes the danger in which he has put himself. It was virtually certain that he would be severely injured.

RANSOM CONQUERS THE EVIL ONE

Despite the certainty of injury or death, Ransom begins to fight. The Un-man taunts him, saying that all who stand up for God eventually recant when they realize that God cannot help them. He mockingly repeats Jesus' words on the cross in their original Aramaic: *"Eloi, Eloi lama sabachthani"* ["My God, My God, why have You forsaken Me?"]. If Jesus could not save Himself in that hour, how could He help Ransom?[29] Undeterred, Ransom joins the battle, fighting with his bare hands. Eventually, the Un-man drags him beneath the sea. After they emerge in a dark cave, Ransom kills the Un-man. He begins to climb toward the surface only to discover that the Un-man has been reanimated. Ransom crushes his head with a stone, accompanied with the invocation.[30] Then he casts the body into a pit of fire to be destroyed.

With the battle complete, Ransom emerges from the cave into a pool of water. There by the pool he eats grapes, sleeps, and recovers his strength. Soon, Ransom discovers a human bite wound on his heel. Although he cannot remember when he received the wound, it is bleeding and will not stop.

Note the Christological parallels. Ransom fought the devil (in a possessed man) on behalf of the first woman. He conquered the evil one after hearing words from Christ's crucifixion. He was dragged into the dark pit of the earth where he destroyed the enemy. Then he fought his way to the surface. In his struggles, he crushed the head of his enemy, though his own heel was injured (reminiscent of Genesis 3:15). Following his victory, Ransom travels up from the underworld, emerging through a cave. Although he is alive and strong, he continues to bear the scars of his triumph. The identity of Elwin Ransom is quite clear. This can be none other than an image of Christ's redemptive work.

Finally Ransom, who has undergone all these things, climbs to a valley on top of a mountain. There he sees a coffinlike vessel meant to bear him home, which is accompanied by two eldila. The eldila speak to each other, noting Ransom's weaknesses. They realize that he is made of the dust of the earth and that their power could easily destroy him. They marvel that even his best, most noble, thoughts are mingled with sinfulness that they cannot comprehend. Yet they also see the grace that he has received. Maleldil chose to become incarnate in the same type of human body. Ransom is filled with sinful thoughts, but his sins have been forgiven.[31]

Ransom is not Christ, but he is a type of Christ. The salvation that Ransom carried out is only an extension of the salvation won by Christ. He did this work at the bidding of Maleldil and is himself a forgiven sinner. Yet this does not diminish the work of salvation accomplished by Ransom. When the king of Perelandra first speaks, he acknowledges Ransom. He and his descendents will remember what Maleldil had done through him. Because of his work, Ransom is called their Lord, Friend, and even Savior.[32] Ransom is subordinate to Maleldil, but he is exalted above all others as the chief instrument of Maleldil. Ransom was the savior of this world not because he redeemed it but because he prevented evil from taking control of Perelandra.

That Hideous Strength

The third volume of the Space Trilogy reveals the work of Ransom on Thulcandra. The evil goals of Weston, Devine, and the demonic forces that control them are seen on our planet. They plan to create a scientific immortality apart from God, thereby deifying themselves. God confronts this scheme through Elwin Ransom, who now helps to save our planet.

In the six years since Ransom traveled to Malacandra, his station in life has changed. When an Indian mystic warned his sister that England was about to be attacked by a great evil, she provided Ransom with the money to gather a group of people to combat it. They would come to him, and he would serve as the head of this group. At the same time, Ransom changed his name to "Fisher-King," the name of his sister.

This begins to unveil themes from the Arthurian legends. Arthur is, at times, known as the Fisher-King. Ransom takes this name and, indeed, becomes the "Pendragon," another title once used by King Arthur. Lewis suggests that there has been an unbroken line of Pendragons from Arthur to Ransom. The people that Ransom gathers together are, in reality, Logres, the name Arthur gave to the kingdom he captured from demons. As Pendragon, Ransom is the "Director" of the group, though its orders come from his masters, the Oyeresu of the five great planets.[33]

One may easily see the role of Ransom by following the story of Jane Studdock, an unwilling seer who eventually joins Logres. Jane dreams she is in a crypt, which is later discovered to be the crypt of Merlin. She is terrified and wishes someone would let her out. Immediately, she has a vision of a bearded young man coming into the darkness with strength and boldness. She is comforted by the presence, but she does not know who the man is.[34] The anticipation builds.

The source of the evil plans is the National Institute for Coordinated Experiments (N.I.C.E.). As the N.I.C.E. expands, dense fog also expands to cover England. But as Jane goes up to Ransom's house (St. Anne's), she emerges from the fog and sees a different world that is much larger than the one below. She enters St. Anne's and meets Ransom, the deliverer in her dream. He appears ageless to her (a result of his time on Perelandra), and she notes that he seems to be the focus of all the light in the room. This halo of light is evocative of deity. As she looks at him, she imagines that he would be able to support the entire house physically.[35] Indeed, in his weakness, Ransom does support the entire house not physically, but spiritually.

Ransom's appearance conjures images of Arthur and Solomon in Jane's mind. She finds herself thinking of kingship and its connotations of battle, marriage, priesthood, mercy, and power. Ransom embodies these attributes as the Pendragon of Logres. Furthermore, Ransom seems able partially to perceive thoughts and motives. He is aware of much that is happening in people's lives, yet he needs Jane's visions to see what the N.I.C.E. is doing at Belbury. He lives on a simple diet of bread and wine. The closer Jane comes to him, the less her mind is accessible to the evil Professor Frost.[36]

But who is Ransom? He is called the Pendragon of Logres and is the Director of a group of faithful people. Nonetheless, he does not exercise the salvific role he did on Perelandra, though that is part of his identity. Rather, Ransom is the leader of a diverse group and an interpreter of events. He does not personally deliver the Earth, but it is delivered through his leadership. Ransom confronts Merlin at St. Anne's not in his own power, but in the words of the Invocation. Ransom forbids MacPhee to fight because he does not believe; instead, he sends the elderly Professor Dimble, a Christian, into the battle. It is into Ransom's room that the planetary spirits descend to destroy the evil power. In past times, it was impossible for these eldila to come on Earth, the dominion of the Bent Oyarsa (the devil), lest they destroy it. But Ransom had been kidnapped and taken to Malacandra. He learned to speak Old Solar, and in him, the Oyeresu are able to descend upon this earth again. They had unwittingly removed their own protection, bringing about a fate from which God had previously protected them.[37]

This is the role of Ransom in this story. It is far less Christological than in the previous book, yet there is a sense in which it, too, points to Christ. When Christ was on the earth, He worked personally and directly. Following His ascension, He works mediately, that is, empowering and guiding others. In the framework of this narrative, Christ came to Thulcandra and redeemed the world. Working through Ransom, He saved Perelandra. And He saves Thulcandra once more, working through Ransom, who is working through others.

When this last battle is over, Ransom's job on earth is complete. No natural death awaits him in this world. He has gained the immortality that was present in the new world, Perelandra, the world that gave him second birth and nurtured him at her breast.[38] He is taken from this earth by the Oyeresu. Denniston explains that he is being taken to the same place as King Arthur because Arthur Pendragon was taken alive from the Earth. Earlier, Ransom revealed that Arthur is on Perelandra, along with all the other people who did not die: Enoch, Elias, Moses, and Melchisedec. They dwell in the hall of Melchisedec on the cup-shaped land of Abhalljin beyond the seas of Lur. There Ransom will be taken to live until the end of the universe and into the dawning of the new day.[39] As Ransom miraculously arrived on and departed from Perelandra, so he miraculously disappears from Earth when his work is complete. As Christ ascended into heaven, so Ransom is bodily taken from the Earth.

CONCLUSION

The Christology of the Space Trilogy is complex. Maleldil is clearly Christ, while Ransom offers another level of Christological understanding. It is a Christology that heavily emphasizes the incarnation, keeping the two natures of Christ intact. This is naturally less clear in the person of Ransom. Regarding the Trinity, Lewis emphasizes the Second Person at the expense of the First and Third Persons. Indeed, it might be more accurate to speak simply of his Christology because that is the focus of his trinitarian images. The Christology that Lewis expresses is incomplete but largely consistent with orthodoxy. What is unique is its presentation in this mythic form and its parallel presentation on multiple levels.

NOTES

1. C. S. Lewis, *Out of the Silent Planet* (New York: Macmillan, 1965), 68.
2. C. S. Lewis, *That Hideous Strength* (New York: Macmillan, 1946), 318.
3. Lewis, *Silent Planet*, 74, 121.
4. Lewis, *Silent Planet*, 75; C. S. Lewis, *Perelandra* (New York: Macmillan, 1944), 67.
5. Ibid., 121, 122, 142.
6. Lewis, *Perelandra*, 121.
7. Ibid., 148.
8. Ibid., 220.
9. Lewis, *Silent Planet*, 86.
10. Ibid., 68.
11. Lewis, *Perelandra*, 210, 212; Lewis, *Hideous Strength*, 271.
12. Lewis, *Silent Planet*, 68.
13. Lewis, *Perelandra*, 202.
14. Ibid., 216.
15. Lewis, *Hideous Strength*, 225, 229.
16. Ibid., 229, 230.
17. Ibid., 234.
18. Lewis, *Perelandra*, 15.
19. Ibid., 67.
20. Lewis, *Hideous Strength*, 228.
21. Ibid., 377.
22. Lewis, *Perelandra*, 61, 62.
23. Lewis, *Hideous Strength*, 262.
24. Lewis, *Perelandra*, 34.
25. Ibid., 45, 66.
26. Ibid., 142, 143, 146.
27. Ibid., 147.
28. Ibid., 150.
29. Ibid., 153.
30. Ibid., 181.
31. Ibid., 195.
32. Ibid., 208, 222.
33. Lewis, *Hideous Strength*, 114, 369, 115.
34. Ibid., 136.

35. Ibid., 138, 142, 143.
36. Ibid., 143, 146, 149, 160.
37. Ibid., 290, 291.
38. Ibid., 288, 367.
39. Ibid., 368, 274.

Chapter Six

The Dark Tower

Elwin Ransom traveled to two different planets, prevented Perelandra's fall into sin, and led Logres to defeat the powers of evil on Earth. In the end, he was transported back to Perelandra to live until the end of time. The Space Trilogy ended, leaving readers hungry for more. Might there be more to the story? To their disappointment, Lewis published no further works of science fiction. Following Lewis's death, however, word of a fourth novel began to spread. According to Walter Hooper, the January after C. S. Lewis died, Warren Lewis began to burn many of his brother's personal papers. Hooper happened upon the scene and rescued many of them from destruction.[1] Among them Hooper found 62 handwritten pages of *The Dark Tower*. This manuscript, which is missing two pages and ends midsentence, appears to be a continuation of the Space Trilogy.

In *The Dark Tower*, C. S. Lewis himself joins Elwin Ransom and MacPhee from the Space Trilogy. A scientist named Dr. Orfieu has invented a "chronoscope." Orfieu, Ransom, and MacPhee initially believe that the device allows them to look forward or backward in time, but they soon discover that they are viewing a parallel universe. They see a tyrannical society where people are transformed into automata after being stung by a strange man. "Othertime" appears to be geographically similar to their own world and contains similar-looking people. Orfieu's assistant, Scudamour, learns that his own double is a sinister "Stingingman." At one point, he unwittingly changes places with the Stingingman and finds himself living in Othertime. Scudamour explores this parallel world and the Dark Tower. The narrative ends abruptly as he is reading about temporal mechanics in the tower's library.

The publication of *The Dark Tower* has proven to be quite controversial. Some have welcomed this manuscript, exploring possible plot developments and themes. Others are offended by apparent sexual imagery. Still others consider the writing inferior and unworthy of Lewis. Some have even proposed that a fraud has been perpetrated in the publication of an inauthentic work.[2] While these objections must be taken seriously, it is possible that *The Dark Tower* is indeed a genuine work. Assuming its authenticity, this manuscript provides a rare glimpse into Lewis's unedited literary method. It also suggests several latent Christological themes. Yet even if it is genuine, we need to remember that it was neither completed nor published by Lewis. For these reasons, *The Dark Tower* must be viewed with a degree of suspicion. We cautiously pursue its themes and should consider them subordinate to those in the rest of Lewis's works.

As we examine this partial manuscript, several themes emerge. It is clear that this story involved a critique of totalitarianism. While Lewis's world saw the spread of Nazism and fascism, this novel shows the corruption of a dictatorship. This corruption is also seen in a world filled with images of perverse sexuality. While the sexual references in this manuscript make many people uncomfortable, they demonstrate the depravity of this society. Lewis may also have intended this book to provide a critique of higher education, insofar as the plot centers on Cambridge. Similar ideas can be found in *The Abolition of Man* and *That Hideous Strength*. One theme, however, is significant to this study. In this manuscript, it appears that Lewis was exploring Antichrist figures through two images. The first is the image of a unicorn. The second is an idol depicted as many bodies under one head. Each of these images has significant implications for Lewis's intent because they suggest Antichrist figures.

THE UNICORN

The image of the unicorn is presented through the Stingingman. This unattractive man has a yellow pallor, black hair and a black beard, and is dressed in the darkest robes imaginable. His behavior and appearance evoke images of death, but his most notable feature is a stinger that protruded from his forehead and is likened to a unicorn's horn.[3] Observers from our world refer to him most often as the Stingingman, but it appears that the inhabitants of Othertime are more accustomed to calling him the Unicorn. Camilla identifies him as Lord and makes it clear that he is in control of the Dark Tower. Her words also make it evident that there are unicorns in other geographic regions.[4]

Camilla is not alone in calling the Stingingman Lord. His attendants also address him with this title.[5] What's more, the Unicorn is honored and worshiped. When Scudamour's double first became a unicorn, he experienced an immediate change in status. Not realizing the double had been transformed, one man swaggered into the double's room, boldly cracking a whip. When this man saw that the double had become a unicorn, he prostrated himself, hid his eyes with his hand, and backed out of the room.[6] Even Camilla notes the change, addressing the double as Lord and not by his natural name. She explains that it is illegal to speak to a unicorn as if he were only a common man. That former life is now irrelevant.[7]

The unicorns are the highest caste encountered in this depraved society. They enslave subjects with their stings and direct their activity, and they are worshiped. One more element needs to be mentioned. At one point, Scudamour tries to say, "Thank God," but he finds that he cannot find the words in the language of Othertime for this common phrase.[8] Although there is a word for the lordship of the unicorns, there appears to be no word to address "God."

C. S. Lewis would not have chosen unicorn imagery lightly. He was well-versed in ancient mythology and knew that the unicorn was frequently thought to typify Christ. Consider this passage from *The Discarded Image* in which Lewis writes about medieval conceptions of the earth and its inhabitants, particularly the medieval view of beasts. He writes of one medieval author:

> One of the most remarkable things about Isidore is that he draws no morals from his beasts and gives them no allegorical interpretations. He says the Pelican revives its young by its own blood (XII, vii, 26) but draws no such

parallel between this and the life-giving death of Christ as was later to produce the tremendous *Pie Pelicane*. He tells us from unnamed "writers on the nature of animals" (XII, ii, 13) that the unicorn is a beast too strong for any hunter to take; but if you set a virgin before him he loses all his ferocity, lays down his head in her lap, and sleeps. Then we can kill him. It is hard to believe that any Christian can think for long about this exquisite myth without seeing in it an allegory of the Incarnation and Crucifixion. Yet Isidore makes no such suggestion.[9]

Isidore may not have made the connection between the unicorn and Christ, but Lewis certainly did. It is implausible to think that he would use this imagery—indeed, the very name of the mythical beast—without some connection to Christ.

We see further evidence of this in Lewis's poem "The Late Passenger." As rain falls on the already loaded ark, an animal knocks on the door. Noah calls to his sons to let it in, but not wanting to make any more work for themselves, they claim the noise is something else. Noah emerges to see the beast flee and laments its departure. He apologizes for the lack of hospitality shown by his sons, wondering if this noble animal will find a stable or a manger on such a night. Lewis reflects that, tragically, many years and much suffering would pass before the Unicorn would again present Himself at a stable and a manger. Only then would He give humanity the gifts that He might have given to Noah and his family.[10]

The unicorn is a type of Christ. Lewis named *The Dark Tower*'s diabolical figure the "Unicorn Man." At the same time, figures in the two worlds are not interchangeable. Earth's Scudamour is a decent human being, but his double is a monster. So we might suppose that the Unicorn Man, though employing imagery that belongs to Christ in our world, is not meant to be Christ but is intended to be something entirely different—the negation of Christ.

THE DIABOLICAL HEAD

There is another figure of the Antichrist in *The Dark Tower*. Victims who are brought before the Stingingman are first led before an idol. They are told that as they pray to him, he will come from behind them, lay his hands on them, and breathe his life into them. They are unaware that it is the Stingingman who actually transforms them.[11] As sinister as this picture is, the description of the idol evokes even more corruption. This idol is made up of numerous nude human bodies joined together under one large head. Both male and female bodies are depicted, though, in many cases, their anatomy is distorted. Far from being an erotic or sensual image, this idol appears repulsive. All of these bodies, which the artist apparently despised, were joined together with one enormous head.[12]

The idea that the idol consists of many bodies with one head is the antithesis of New Testament images of Christ as head of the body—His church (see, for example, 1 Corinthians 11:13; Ephesians 1:10; Colossians 1:18). Here, however, the image is unpleasant. The idol does not express a love or appreciation of humanity, but it seems to be designed to mock it. The deity of Othertime is antithetical to Christ.

In *That Hideous Strength*, Lewis presents another diabolical vision that involves a head. There he employs a severed human head through which spiritual forces communicate. In *The Dark Tower*, a head of many grotesque bodies is the image of the evil deity. In both cases, the image is a perversion of the headship of Christ.

CONCLUSION

In the end, the reader is left to speculate about this book. Lewis did not publish it, nor did he seek its publication. It is unfinished and rough, but it presents some interesting possibilities. What did Lewis intend to accomplish with this work? One need only look at the completed volumes of the Space Trilogy to see the embryonic themes fully developed. While *The Dark Tower* is not a work that will appeal to the general reader, it shows more of Lewis's creative thought and vision. Lewis's theology, in mythical terms, is present, though undeveloped.

NOTES

1. The story of this bonfire is found in abbreviated form in Hooper's preface to C. S. Lewis, *The Dark Tower and Other Stories*, ed. Walter Hooper (New York: Harcourt, Brace, Jovanovich, 1977), 7.
2. Arguments against the authenticity of *The Dark Tower* are well artic-

ulated in Kathryn Lindskoog, *Sleuthing C. S. Lewis: More Light in the Shadowlands* (Macon, Ga.: Mercer University Press, 2001).

3. Lewis, *Dark Tower*, 33.

4. Ibid., 65.

5. Ibid., 73.

6. Ibid., 43–44.

7. Ibid., 66.

8. Ibid., 65.

9. C. S. Lewis, *The Discarded Image* (Cambridge: Cambridge University Press, 1964), 149–50.

10. C. S. Lewis, "The Late Passenger," in *The Collected Poems of C. S. Lewis* (London: Fount Paperbacks, 1994), 61–62.

11. Lewis, *Dark Tower*, 69.

12. Ibid., 31.

Chapter Seven

The Screwtape Letters

On Sunday, July 15, 1940, as he was leaving the 8 A.M. Communion service at Holy Trinity Church in Headington Quarry, C. S. Lewis thought of an idea for a book. It would be a collection of letters from an older, more experienced devil to a neophyte.[1] Those letters were first serialized in a Christian newspaper and later published together as *The Screwtape Letters*. While this account of the genesis of *The Screwtape Letters* might lead one to question the nature of the homily in Headington Quarry that week, it is indicative of the nature of Lewis's thought processes. He continually pondered thematic ideas and developed those he considered to be fruitful. This process led to ideas that arrived at unexpected times.

Once the idea took root, Lewis quickly embraced the task and produced a one-sided correspondence from an older devil, Screwtape, to Wormwood, his nephew. Wormwood has recently completed his demonic training and has been assigned his first human subject. His task is to secure the damnation of this young man. Through these letters, Lewis discusses hell, the devil, and demons and their work on earth, including temptation, war, and suffering. None of these subjects is unusual, but the approach of *The Screwtape Letters* makes the reader consider them anew. While Screwtape instructs Wormwood in the art of securing his victim for hell, Lewis reveals what he considers to be some of the varied methods of the demons.

The Screwtape Letters addresses many themes prevalent in Lewis's other works, but the tone is profoundly different. Here he bridges the gap between his literary and apologetic writings. Unlike his apologetic works, here Lewis does not attempt to prove his theological points; he simply states them through Screwtape. This method makes the reader less likely to focus on the mechanics of the intellectual arguments and more likely to consider the content. Consequently, readers who may have balked at some of Lewis's apologetics, or who have bristled over what they consider to be false dichotomies or straw arguments, have enjoyed *The Screwtape Letters*. At the same time, Lewis never compromises or conceals his beliefs. The reader will not easily overlook the points of the book.

REVERSED PERSPECTIVE

The reader must, however, understand the nature of *The Screwtape Letters*. It is a confusing work for some because it is written entirely from a diabolical point of view. At best, human beings are subjects to be influenced and controlled. At worst, they are merely a source of food for demons. This demonic point of view is consistent throughout the book. Nowhere does Lewis interject narrative comments, but he allows his point to be made by Screwtape. He does this so thoroughly that some readers question his intent. When it was first serialized, one reader complained that much of the advice given in these letters seemed not only erroneous, but positively diabolical.[2] While this reader misunderstood the book, he certainly comprehended Screwtape's arguments. Lewis meticulously portrays a hell that mimics heaven but completely reverses the standards. As Christians refer to our heavenly Father, the demons speak of their Father below. The name "Satan" means "adversary," but in *The Screwtape Letters,* God is consistently referred to as the enemy. Hell appears to be extremely bureaucratic, but this administration is not a hierarchy; instead, it is a "lowerarchy." Because heaven is sometimes described as the beatific vision, hell is gleefully called the "miserific vision." Screwtape is repulsed at the words of Psalm 16:11, which promise eternal pleasures at God's right hand. Similarly, hell reverses heaven's behavior. In a perverse sacramental parody, hell wants to win souls so they can be consumed. Should Wormwood fail in this task, he himself will be devoured by other demons hungry for destruction.[3] The extent to which this reversed perspective has been carried out is a major key to the success of *The Screwtape Letters*. Lewis has created a seamless presentation of hell and done so with wit, insight, and character.

THE RESPONSES OF READERS

These very things, which are signs of the literary integrity for which Lewis strove, also give rise to varied responses from readers. Screwtape propelled Lewis to the fame that he holds to this day. Readers of Lewis's books often begin with *The Screwtape Letters*. Many authors have attempted duplication or additions to the letters. But not all readers hold the book in such high regard. Some consider the book to be difficult reading not because of the writing but because of the subject matter. Reading about the schemes of demons and satanic assault on humanity is dreary work. Lewis reflects this feeling in his 1960 preface, saying that writing this book was difficult work. Screwtape's words needed to be devoid of goodness, beauty, and other virtues. This is a dark and oppressive state of mind that could not be endured by Lewis for long periods of time.[4]

While reactions are varied, these reactions testify to the effectiveness of *The Screwtape Letters*. Those who exalt the book demonstrate an awareness of the Christian content of the letters. Readers who find the subject difficult have clearly been affected by the letters' warnings of the reality and possible methods of devils.

LEWIS'S BELIEF IN DEMONOLOGY

Another explanation of the success of this book is that Lewis writes of something that is more than a literary construct. He firmly believed in the reality of devils—and specifically in the reality of a personal devil. Yet he does not go to great lengths to prove this belief. He determines the scope and nature of his presentation. In doing so, he assumes the reality of demons, neither defending nor proving their existence but simply describing their activity. While he displays great creativity in his examination of demonic methods, Lewis does not stray far from traditional understanding of these topics.

One error he purposefully avoids is dualism. In his preface to the 1960 edition, Lewis addresses both the existence and nature of devils. He does this because he was often asked if he believed in Satan. He emphatically denies belief in a self-existent, eternal power that is the opposite of God. That is not the Christian teaching. God is unique; He has no opposite. Lewis then states that he does believe in devils—including Satan.[5] Lewis does not simply reject dualism, but he shows the true opposite of the devil—the archangel Michael. Likewise, hell is not a mirror image of heaven; instead, it is a mockery. There can be no absolute reverse of heaven because God, the focus of heaven, has no opposite.

Finally, Lewis cautions the reader who approaches this book, warning him or her throughout the entire collection of letters, as well as more directly in the preface, that there are two common errors that humans make regarding the devils. First, some humans do not believe in their existence, thereby ignoring a grave danger. Second, an equally dangerous error is to be overly interested in devils and, consequently, to pay them too much attention. Either error can serve the demonic cause.[6]

Lewis never intended to encourage either error. The writing, which he found gritty and difficult, can also be difficult for the reader. It is helpful for Christians to know demonic tactics; to show excessive interest would be most unhealthy.

CHRISTOLOGY IN *THE SCREWTAPE LETTERS*

The Screwtape Letters is a theological work, and Lewis's theology is revealed in a diabolical negation of truth. Still, Christological material is sparse, and the person and work of Jesus Christ receive little attention in this book. It would appear that here, as in some of his other writings, Lewis simply assumes what he believes to be orthodox Christology and writes on topics that interest him. There are, however, some notable passages that reveal his Christology. Through Screwtape, Lewis writes of the incarnation, of demonic reaction to salvation, and of the quest for the historical Jesus.

THE INCARNATION

In three separate passages, Screwtape discusses the incarnation. The first discussion takes place in his initial letter to Wormwood. Screwtape cautions his nephew against using argument to keep the subject away from God. Although logical argument was once effective, it should not be used today because, through it, the subject might make a fuller use of reason and thus see the rationality of the Christian faith. Instead, the subject is to be directed to feelings and to a desire for novelty and immediate sensory experiences. Wormwood is ignorant of these basic facts, something that Screwtape ascribes to the demonic nature. Unlike a human, Wormwood is pure spirit, thus he cannot understand all human feelings. As Screwtape says this, he notes that Christ's incarnation is God's "abominable advantage."[7] Here Lewis reflects Hebrews 4:15: "For we do not have a high priest who is unable to sympathize with our weaknesses, but we have one who has been tempted in every way, just as we are—yet was without sin." If God has truly taken on human flesh and has undergone human experiences, He can understand and sympathize with human weaknesses.

Later, while discussing prayer, Screwtape says that the subject will envision

> images derived from pictures of the Enemy as He appeared during the discreditable episode known as the Incarnation; there will be vaguer—perhaps quite savage and puerile images associated with the other two Persons.[8]

A demon considers the incarnation to be discreditable. The goal of this particular letter is to focus the human subject's attention on the ridiculous things that are passing through his thoughts. Screwtape's advice is to adopt a double-edged attack. The subject should be shown the folly of praying to a person and the silliness of his images of the First and Third Persons of the Trinity. From a demonic point of view, there is no appropriate image for prayer. The consternation of the devils also demonstrates what, for Lewis, was an important effect of the incarnation. While human images of the Father may be inappropriately anthropomorphic and images of the Holy Spirit are often nebulous at best, it *is* possible to visualize the incarnate Son of God. His humanity makes Him accessible.

Screwtape's reference to the incarnation as a discreditable episode does not mean that Lewis viewed the incarnation as a temporary state or an adoption of human nature for a limited period. The most forceful reference to Christ occurs in the last letter in the collection. Wormwood's subject is killed in an air raid and dies as a Christian. Screwtape tells his nephew that as the human subject died, he not only saw God's protecting angels but Christ Himself. The presence of God, which is agonizing torment to the demons, is revealed to the human subject. Because he believed in Christ, he is able to see God Himself because God has assumed a human nature.[9] Even in heaven, Christ remains incarnate and, furthermore, remains accessible and comprehensible to the human subject. As the demons bemoan their loss of this human being, they continue the theme begun in the first letter—that physical corporeality is inferior to being pure spirit. Here they continue to denigrate the incarnation while also ridiculing any human nature. The victim that they failed to capture is reviled as an animal, begotten in a bed. But God has revealed Himself to such creatures, and it is this "animal nature" that was assumed by the divine Son. Lewis's brief presentation of the incarnation is a restatement of orthodox Christology. What is novel is his application of the teaching, including the possible demonic reaction to these sacred mysteries.

SATANIC REACTION TO SALVATION

In a brief discussion of salvation, the reader again can consider demonic reaction to Christian dogma. Screwtape struggles to make sense of God's plan for human beings. What does God want to do with humans? The demons claim that this was the chief issue that led to the fall of Satan. God created humanity, foreseeing the fall into sin and knowing that He would need to redeem them on a cross. How could He do such a thing? Satan could not understand a love so deep and so giving that God would still choose to create and sustain humanity, knowing the pain they would cause Him.[10] God's incomprehensible love is a pivotal theme of this book. Screwtape repeatedly writes of God's love and is confident that it is fraudulent. He is convinced that God must be concealing an ulterior motive. Nowhere is this issue so prevalent as in this letter. Satan does not understand why God would want to redeem His fallen creation. The devil cannot accept the explanation of love.

Lewis offers no theory of how the atonement might be effective. He does not postulate how, or even why, God foresaw the crucifixion. He simply states that God had foreseen it. The crucifixion was not an accidental occurrence, but it was part of God's foreknown and forechosen plan, which is utterly perplexing to the demons.

THE QUEST FOR THE HISTORICAL JESUS

Screwtape has nothing but scorn for God. He ridicules the Christ, the incarnation, and His passion, but Screwtape is not ignorant of theology. Screwtape's longest consideration of Jesus Christ demonstrates an awareness of modern theological trends. Through the words of a demon, Lewis rebukes modern theology as Screwtape turns his attention to the quest for the historical Jesus.

Unlike other theological issues, Screwtape speaks favorably of this endeavor, saying that it is essential and has been promoted by demons. By this point in the letters, the human subject has become a Christian. Because Screwtape has given up hope that they will be able to destroy the subject's faith, he encourages Wormwood to corrupt it. He is to foster the idea that there once was a simple, purer form of Christianity. Wormwood is to teach that, early in its history, the Christian religion began altering the teachings of Jesus. The solution is to remove these alleged additions and changes, thereby returning to the "original" Christianity.[11] Naturally, such an effort is not based on the biblical texts or upon objective evidence. It is, rather, grounded in an individual's subjective opinion of what Christianity should be. Screwtape's strategy is an accurate, if simplistic, characterization of the quest for the historical Jesus. As the letter continues, Screwtape explains that in the last generation, the demons promoted a "historical Jesus" who reflected liberal and humanitarian ideals. At the time he wrote the letter, Screwtape said the demons were encouraging a new version of "Jesus" based on Marxian, revolutionary ideas.[12] An appraisal of modern theology does indeed reveal such emphases. The letter then states that the demons intend to change these constructions approximately every 30 years. Whether one accepts or rejects Lewis's judgment that the origin of these quests is demonic, it is easy to see multiplication of alternative Christological paradigms. However, Lewis was overly cautious in estimating a 30-year interval. Today little time passes between theological fads.

Screwtape details the demonic benefits of these quests. First, they direct human devotion toward something that does not exist because each historical Jesus is really ahistorical; they reflect the current culture rather than the texts on which they are supposedly based. Indeed, Screwtape continues, because the documents cannot be added to (an assumption that holds less weight today than it did when Lewis first wrote the letter), each historical Jesus is discovered by suppressing certain texts, overemphasizing others, and simply guessing at other points. If such an ahistorical Jesus is substituted for the Jesus of the Bible, the object of devotion is called into question and, ultimately, the devotion itself will fade.

Second, each of these theories stresses its particular issue over all else. The result is that humanity is distracted from considering who Jesus really is and what He has done for us. As one particular aspect of Jesus is emphasized, He is seen solely as a teacher. At the same time, the demons want the similarities among Jesus and other great moral teachers to be obscured.[13] The demons do not want the human subject to listen to any moral teacher, and Jesus is a moral teacher (though not merely a teacher). While Lewis does not present, in this letter, his argument regarding why Jesus could not be merely a moral teacher, he is laying the foundation for that argument as it is expressed in his other works. Here, it is simply stated that when Jesus is presented merely as teacher, His true person and work are eclipsed. There is, indeed, much to commend this argument. Transitory issues and causes have repeatedly captivated theology; distraction remains a dangerous possibility, and Lewis attributes it to demons.

Third, Screwtape asserts that, with these constructions, devotional life is destroyed.

> For the real presence of the Enemy, otherwise experienced by prayer and sacrament, we substitute a merely probable, remote, shadowy, and uncouth figure, one who spoke a strange language and died a long time ago. Such an object cannot in fact be worshiped.[14]

Once uncertainty has been introduced into the central articles of the faith, piety may decrease. How is a person to know what to believe when every special interest presents its own Jesus and each construct contradicts the next?

Finally, Screwtape presents what Lewis considers to be the greatest fallacy of the search for the historical Jesus. This effort reads the Gospels simply as biographical or historical documents. The demons rejoice that few people have ever been brought to faith by reading the Gospels in this way. Instead, the earliest converts to Christianity had a different experience. They were already aware of their own sinfulness. They were converted when they encountered the historical truth of Christ's resurrection and the redemption that He accomplished. Indeed, people were brought to faith in this way even before the Gospels had been written.[15]

The intent of the Gospels, in Lewis's view, is not to provide a biography of Jesus. Faith does not come through reading a reconstructed biography, either real or imagined, but through an encounter with the facts of the resurrection and redemption. All else is supportive of these.

CONCLUSION

The Screwtape Letters reveals a small portion of Lewis's Christology, a portion presented in negative terms from the mouth of a demon. Still, it is representative of much of his thinking. The incarnation and resurrection are central and are considered to be historical facts. The doctrine of the redemption is mentioned but in a manner typical of other writings, with no explanation of how it is effective. As in other works, modern theology is rebuked for straying from the basics of mere Christianity. While some of the situations faced by the human subject are no longer applicable to modern people, *The Screwtape Letters* remains a popular work because the basic approach of the book continues to resonate with readers. This book captures the imagination and, having captured it, communicates Lewis's theology.

NOTES

1. Roger Lancelyn Green, and Walter Hooper, *C. S. Lewis: A Biography* (New York: Harcourt, Brace, Jovanovich, 1974), 191.
2. Cited in Colin Duriez, *The C. S. Lewis Handbook* (Grand Rapids: Baker, 1990), 181.
3. C. S. Lewis, *The Screwtape Letters* (New York: Macmillan, 1961), 91, 101, 141, 149.

4. Ibid., xiv.
5. Ibid., 1960 preface, vii.
6. Ibid., 1961 preface, 3.
7. Ibid., 8–9.
8. Ibid., 22.
9. Ibid., 148.
10. Ibid., 86.
11. Ibid., 106ff.
12. Ibid., 106.
13. Ibid., 107.
14. Ibid.
15. Ibid., 108.

Chapter Eight

The Great Divorce

Three years after *The Screwtape Letters*, C. S. Lewis published another book that took readers to the edge of hell. This time, however, we hear the words not of demons but of humans. These souls receive a brief respite from their torment and travel to the borders of heaven where they speak with the faithful. Although they are offered one final opportunity to be saved, only one remains in heaven, while the rest choose to return to hell. The conversations reveal their tragic rejection of God's gift of salvation.

Lewis is careful to remind his readers that this is fiction and not a literal description of the afterlife. While the story clearly has spiritual applications, it is not intended to be an accurate portrayal of anything occurring after death.[1] The final scene of the book reinforces this by claiming that the events were seen in a dream. Nonetheless, Lewis presents theological themes in this medium. Through most of his writings, Lewis tried to limit himself to teachings held in common by the majority of Christians, but this book deals, in part, with purgatory. This disputed doctrine is not part of mere Christianity, and it may disturb some readers. Lewis has, however, altered some of the details to make purgatory fit more harmoniously in this narrative. The traditional depiction of purgatory is of a place for those who will eventually be in heaven; Lewis believed that souls went to purgatory to be purified before they entered eternal paradise. In this story, however, the souls live in a middle ground from which some will go to heaven and some to hell. Lewis did not believe this was an accurate portrayal, but he used it to support his narrative. Although Lewis believed in purgatory, this book makes it clear that the conversations overheard are fictional and depict choices that are made on earth during this life.

Lewis provides an interesting depiction of the afterlife, but he does not truly offer descriptions of heaven or hell. The narrative begins in the "grey city." For the moment, this place is in a state of perpetual twilight. It is impermanent and devoid of true pleasure, but it is not yet hell. Eventually, the twilight will turn into the eternal darkness of hell. Until then, some souls are able to leave this city, but afterward, they will be unable to leave. The grey city is insubstantial, only a parody of reality. Earth is somewhat more substantial, but heaven is the realm of absolute reality. The residents of the grey city cannot bear the solidness of heaven. They look like ghosts and are unable to interact with the reality of heaven. We see this when a ghost attempts to take with him one apple from paradise because he wants solid matter to sell in the grey city. He somehow picks up one small apple and tries to return to the grey city, but he is stopped. He is acting foolishly. The apple, in all its solid reality, cannot fit in hell. Hell simply is not large enough to hold even one heavenly apple. Instead, the man is encouraged to stay and learn to eat these real apples.[2] The same thought is echoed later in the book as hell is described as so insubstantial that it is smaller than a pebble on earth. It is even smaller than a single atom in heaven, the real world.[3] While earth is tiny, insubstantial, and shadowy in comparison to heaven, hell is worse. It is the absence of reality. Where Christ is—heaven—there is reality because He is the highest reality, the ultimate truth and substance.

CHRISTOLOGY IN *THE GREAT DIVORCE*

For all its creative approaches to the afterlife, the scarcity of Christological material in *The Great Divorce* is surprising. Indeed, the lack of material about God in general is amazing. Essential Christian teachings are simply assumed in this work. Much of this book focuses on souls who have no real interest in Christ; thus, He is absent from the dialogue. Yet there are some significant reflections of Christology.

THE DESCENT INTO HELL

The most significant Christological discussion in this book involves Christ's descent into hell. Lewis arrives at this topic from a discussion of the insubstantial size of hell. The narrator asks if it would not be possible for one of the solid people (the blessed souls) to enter the grey city to persuade its denizens to come to heaven. The narrator soon learns that the solid people would not fit in hell. They are not capable of reducing themselves to fit within its confines. This is not true of God, however. He is the only one truly capable of lowering Himself into the confines of hell. Hearing this, the narrator asks if the Lord will descend into hell once again to reach these people. He perceives the descent into hell as a time-bound event. Since the work of Jesus was completed, more people have entered hell. Would God repeat His descent for their good? The heavenly guide challenges this understanding of time. Time is part of our earthly experience, but it does function in the same manner outside of creation. So the descent into hell occurred outside of our timeline. Because of this

> "[a]ll moments that have been or shall be were, or are, present in the moment of His descending. There is no spirit in prison to whom He did not preach."
>
> "And some hear him?"
>
> "Aye."[4]

In the descent, as Lewis presents it, Christ appears to preach to the "spirits in prison" (1 Peter 3:19–20). Lewis frees the descent from the constraints of time and history. Because time is a part of God's creation, events outside of our world are also outside of time. Because of this, all the spirits in prison, regardless of when they lived and died, have the opportunity to hear Christ at His descent. There is no question of fairness in who did or did not hear the preaching of Christ. Lewis's understanding applies His preaching to all. Everyone in hell had, or will have, the opportunity to hear Christ. With hearing comes the possibility of belief. Yet Lewis does not maintain that everyone will listen to Christ. While this is possible, damnation likewise is a tragic possibility. While God does not desire the damnation of any human, He will not compel anyone to receive salvation. Any person is able to choose eternal death and reject eternal life. Their request will, sadly, be granted.[5]

THE BLEEDING CHARITY

The descent into hell is by far the most explicit Christological doctrine in *The Great Divorce*, but it is by no means the only depiction of Christ. One of the more powerful passages is found in the dialogue between an argumentative man from the grey city and a murderer who is in heaven. The ghost protests the presence of the murderer and asks about his victim. The ghost is told that the victim is in heaven as well (though "deeper" in paradise). At this news, the ghost grows belligerent. He cannot understand why he has been in the grey city while a murderer has been in paradise. The ghost protests,

"I'm asking for nothing but my rights." . . .

"Oh no. It's not so bad as that. I haven't got my rights, or I should not be here. You will not get yours either. You'll get something far better. Never fear." . . .

"I only want my rights. I'm not asking for anybody's bleeding charity."

"Then do. At once. Ask for the Bleeding Charity. Everything is here for the asking and nothing can be bought."[6]

Reliance on rights is hopeless when eternal salvation is in the balance. The ghost has nothing to offer before God. He wasn't a decent person. He did not do his best. He, like the rest of humanity, failed. According to rights, we deserve damnation; instead, God graciously gives us salvation. While pride may make one reluctant to accept charity, charity is the only hope. This love is no abstraction. Lewis personifies it in Christ. When the ghost objects to "bleeding charity," the other replies, "Ask for the Bleeding Charity." The love of Christ is seen in His passion, literally in His bleeding charity.

THE SUFFERING GOD

Another of the souls from the grey city is a mother who had lost her son. She speaks of a mother's love and how she has suffered at the absence of her son. She thinks that reunion with him would end her suffering. It becomes clear, however, that she desires her son above all else. She seeks heaven not for the sake of God, but only to see her son. When the guide shows the inadequacy of her desire, she protests that she loved her son. Living apart from him has caused her to suffer. The guide responds that she is not alone in these things. God also loves. He has suffered, and He has patiently waited—not only for one but for countless people.[7]

Lewis connects Christ's suffering with human suffering. The heavenly guide does not deny the mother's suffering or waiting (though he does show deficiencies in it). Instead, he points her through her suffering to another. Lewis considers the woman self-possessed. Because she needs to move away from herself, she is directed to the suffering of Christ. But focus on His passion does not ignore her suffering. He *also* loves, suffers, and waits, but He waits for her. Christ's suffering does not remove present human suffering nor eliminate affliction in this life. Yet humanity is not alone in suffering because the incarnate God knows what it is to suffer. Indeed, Lewis does not restrict Christ's suffering to one time, but he speaks of it in the present tense. A Christian may suffer, but she will not be alone in suffering because Christ also suffers.

PRAISES SUNG TO CHRIST

Another striking passage occurs at the salvation of one of the souls who has been carrying a lizard on his shoulder—a symbol of lust. After some time, the man agrees to let his heavenly guide kill the lizard so he might remain in heaven. As the guide does this (and it is a painful event), the lizard is transformed into a solid and beautiful horse—no longer lust but holy desire. At the same time, the ghostly man becomes substantial. In response, heaven itself rejoices, the land breaking into song. The song[8] is clearly based on Psalm 110:

> The LORD says to my Lord: "Sit at My right hand until I make Your enemies a footstool for Your feet." The LORD will extend Your mighty scepter from Zion; You will rule in the midst of Your enemies. Your troops will be willing on Your day of battle. Arrayed in holy majesty, from the womb of the dawn You will receive the dew of Your youth. The LORD has sworn and will not change His mind: "You are a priest forever, in the order of Melchizedek." The Lord

is at Your right hand; He will crush kings on the day of His
wrath. He will judge the nations, heaping up the dead and
crushing the rulers of the whole earth. He will drink from
a brook beside the way; therefore, He will lift up His head.

This highly messianic psalm is frequently cited in the New
Testament. Christ uses it as a demonstration of His deity in
Matthew 22:41–46. He particularly focuses on the opening words,
"The LORD says to my Lord," and asks the Pharisees to explain
how David can call his descendent "Lord." The Pharisees were
unable to answer this question because they denied the deity of
Christ. Lewis picks up this same theme in his own psalm of praise,
substituting the title "Master" for "Lord." The effect is virtually
identical to the original psalm, reflecting the First and Second Persons of the Trinity.

The psalm continues with an invitation for his Lord to sit at
the LORD's right hand. The image of sitting at God's right hand, as
reflected in Scripture and the creeds, connotes a position of divine
honor, power, and authority. Lewis conveys the same concepts
with new language, saying that the master is called up into the
heavens by His Master, where He is given rest, splendor, and
authority. It is interesting to see that, once again, as he deals with
a biblical and creedal doctrine that may confuse some readers,
Lewis does not go to great lengths to explain it. He assumes the
accuracy of his image of the right hand of God and subtly
expresses it.

The psalmist notes that the enemies of the Lord will be made
a footstool for His feet—an image that communicated dominion
and power in the ancient East. Here, Lewis greatly expands and
opens the images. In the case of the man who had been controlled
by his lust, the enemy is readily apparent. This sinfulness was
specifically conquered and, after being killed, was transformed
into the very thing it was originally intended to be—holy desire.
The corrupt, sinful nature had been subjugated to the will of God
and was now restored to its goodness. Yet Lewis does not restrict
this work to the one man. It also applies to all God's people. In
this more generic sense, the enemies are depersonalized and dealt
with in greater detail. Where the psalmist writes of enemies,
Lewis's song refers to any person or nature who had opposed God.
All humanity is included in this subjection because all have been
enemies of God. At the same time, Lewis alters the image of the

footstool. In his version, the enemies are made dancing slaves, backs to ride on, and, in more direct reference to the psalm, things on which God's feet rest. The image moves closer to the present, though it seems to be more a courtly image than a modern one. Where the psalm speaks of the destruction of kings and nations, Lewis softens and personalizes it, seeking not only the vanquishing of other beings, but all people. When the master has also overcome us, we become the people we were intended to be. In this, God seems less vindictive and more benevolent, vanquishing to save. Such an overcoming has just been demonstrated in the salvation of the man and the transformation of lust to holy desire.

Key to the understanding of Psalm 110 is the interpretation of Melchizedek and the permanent, non-Aaronic, priesthood, a motif that is particularly emphasized in the Epistle to the Hebrews. Once again, Lewis includes the themes of the psalm, but he modifies them by deliberately including themes from Hebrews 7. Where the psalmist writes that the Lord is appointed a priest forever, Lewis expands it, saying that He is appointed to be our eternal High Priest and "King of Justice." The letter to the Hebrews has heavily influenced Christian understanding of Psalm 110. In the psalm, the Lord is called a priest. Stressing the supremacy of Jesus to the old covenant, Hebrews names Him High Priest, a title Lewis repeats. However, the title "King of Justice" does mark a sophisticated departure from the psalm. Melchizedek was King of Salem—literally, "king of peace"—yet his name means "king of righteousness." The psalmist notes the justice of the Lord as He judges the nations, yet the theme is never explicitly developed. Lewis includes both justice and peace. His psalm of heaven draws heavily on Psalm 110, but it draws also on his own poetic talents. He has woven a credible psalm of his own that reveals more of the Christ, who is seated at the right hand of God—in rest, honor, and power.

THE PROBLEM OF HELL: RESOLVED

After raising the issue of hell in this book, Lewis must again consider its meaning. What does the existence of hell say about the love and power of God? While this issue troubled Lewis when writing *The Problem of Pain*, here he has resolved it. The solution to this conundrum is free will. God grants some degree of free will to humanity, but free will includes consequences. The ultimate consequence of the abuse of free will is rejection of God and eventual damnation. Thus, Lewis writes,

> There are only two kinds of people in the end: those who say to God, "Thy will be done," and those to whom God says, in the end, "*Thy* will be done." All that are in Hell, choose it. Without that self-choice there could be no Hell.[9]

Hell is ultimately total isolation. The grey city expands in all directions as the souls seek to move away from one another. In the end, total isolation from human beings and God becomes the greatest hell. Does this make heaven and hell only states of mind? The guide says that hell truly is a state of mind. It is a self-chosen isolation from other people and from God Himself. This is not true of heaven. Heaven is pure reality.[10] Indeed, heaven is reality itself, not a mental delusion but the true reality. In contrast, hell is the antithesis of reality; it is tragically self-chosen isolation. This is so pronounced that Lewis describes an all-embracing heaven and hell. From the perspective of eternity, humanity will look back on their life on earth. Those who are saved will see it all as part of heaven. Because God was with them, even earth was blessed. In contrast, the damned will look at their earthly life in misery. They had isolated themselves from God and other people on earth, and they continue to do so for all eternity.[11] The reality of their eternal state will consume their earthly memories—not obliterating them but transforming their understanding. Lewis may have wished for an empty hell, but he was unable to support this idea. If free will has any meaning, it must include the ability to reject the Christ and His salvation. God's grace can indeed be resisted.

REBUKE OF LIBERAL THEOLOGY

In *The Screwtape Letters*, Lewis analyzes liberal theology in general, as well as its search for the historical Jesus. He resumes this criticism in *The Great Divorce* by writing about an apostate bishop who lives in the grey city, still clinging to his empty theology. While the bishop considers his theology to be a triumph, his guide criticizes it as following the spirit of the age. Lewis infuses the scene with dark humor. The heavenly guide provided to the bishop once shared the bishop's ideas but changed his mind in later life. When the bishop criticizes his friend for believing in a literal heaven and hell, the guide is incredulous. The bishop does not yet believe in hell, even after living there. He views the dim illumination of that city not as twilight that signals the approaching night, but as the first light of a new dawn. Instead of admitting that he lives in the fringes of hell, the bishop rationalizes his situation and tries to interpret his environment as heaven. When his guide explains that he was sent to hell because he was apostate, the bishop is shocked. He protests that he took hard positions out of honesty. God had given him a rational mind, and he had used it. When his reason determined that the doctrine of the resurrection was untenable, he had the integrity to deny it openly. In doing this, he risked his reputation. How, then, could he be sent to hell? The guide does not accept this excuse. There was no risk in repeating the unbelief of his culture. The bishop's apostasy boosted his popularity; ultimately, it enhanced his career.[12]

Despite this, the heavenly guide will not give up. He calls the bishop to repentance, faith, and heaven, but the bishop cannot accept. Offered answers to his questions, the bishop wants to continue theological speculation. His guide explains that this is not possible. The bishop is not needed in heaven, but he is wanted and invited to share its joys. There is no place for unbelieving speculation in paradise, where God Himself reveals the true answers. He will be forgiven and truly know God. The guide tries to move the bishop from his self-centered religion to a focus on Christ. While the bishop wants nothing but speculation, in heaven he could find the true answers.[13] Lewis presents a traditional image of heaven. Questions are answered. Living in the presence of Christ, we will see the face of God, who is eternal Fact.

In the end, the bishop is unconvinced. He does not believe in the existence of God, heaven, or hell, but he wants to continue studying theology. In fact, the bishop returns to hell to present a paper at a theological society! The bishop summarizes his paper. It begins by focusing on the relatively young age at which Jesus died. The bishop hypothesizes that if Jesus had lived longer, He would have softened His positions and outgrown some of His earlier views. From this premise, the ghost intends to ask his listeners to speculate about the developing ideas of a more mature Jesus. In light of this, the bishop views Christ's crucifixion to be disastrous. It tragically shortened an otherwise promising theological career. Ironically, while denying the person, work, and teaching of

Christ, the ghostly bishop still reverently bows his head when he speaks the name "Jesus."[14]

The guide does not respond to this blend of external signs of piety and a denial of historic Christianity. The bishop has rejected the gift of heaven. In silence, the guide walks away, and the bishop returns to hell, singing a hymn. Lewis's satire is biting. Many theologians have found themselves rejecting the existence of God and any objective truth. It was such a theological climate that prompted Lewis to popularize and defend traditional Christianity. No one, not even an apostate bishop, is beyond hope of salvation, but ultimately, those who reject God will be damned.

Lewis is adamant in his condemnation of liberal theology. While not as scathing, he also includes a personal caution to more conservative Christians like himself. George MacDonald, his heavenly guide, warns him that all people should beware of the dangerous possibility of rejecting heaven's joys by clinging to one's own presuppositions. He cautions about being so interested in proving God's existence through apologetics that one cares little for God Himself. Others may be so focused on evangelistic outreach that they pay little heed to Christ Himself.[15] These examples are warnings to us. Knowledge is not synonymous with faith. Above all, Christ must be central.

HEAVEN

The Great Divorce focuses on the souls in hell, the choices that put them there, and the possibility of salvation. There is no depiction of hell itself, only a picture of the grey city. Neither is heaven directly seen, at least not "Deep Heaven"; instead, Lewis shows us the fringes of paradise. Yet Lewis gives the reader some glimpses of heaven. Each ghost from the grey city hears of the joys of heaven and is invited to share them, but each ghost must leave hell behind. In the end, only one ghost is willing to do that, at which heaven rejoices, but the rest choose to return to hell.

In one of the conversations, a ghost asks about the purpose of our existence. Her guide responds that we were born so our God can give us infinite happiness. It is available for anyone who will receive it.[16] That is the invitation. If abuse of free will allows one to choose hell, it is still God's wish that all should gain heaven, and He has made that possible through Jesus Christ.

CONCLUSION

At the end of *The Great Divorce*, dawn comes to the fringes of heaven. It may be presumed that, at the same time, night falls on the grey city. At that moment, the narrator wakes from his dream and the book ends. This was only a dream not a description of real events in the afterlife. The dialogue between the residents of the grey city and those of heaven took place on earth. The choices shown there had already been made here.

The events themselves are fictitious, but the message is not. Neither the choices made by the souls nor the doctrines of the person of Christ are modified for the narrative—only framed within its words. While a complete discussion of the person and work of Christ is not provided in *The Great Divorce*, it does contain images that illuminate Lewis's Christology. Christ is revealed as the Bleeding Charity, the Suffering God, and the Life-Giver. He descended into hell to preach to the spirits in prison, and He is seated at the right hand of God in power and glory. Above all, the invitation to heaven's bliss is heard.

NOTES

1. C. S. Lewis, *The Great Divorce* (New York: Macmillan, 1946), preface, 7–8.
2. Ibid., 52.
3. Ibid., 122.
4. Ibid., 123–24.
5. Ibid., 124.
6. Ibid., 33–35.
7. Ibid., 92.
8. Ibid., 103–4.
9. Ibid., 72.
10. Ibid., 69.
11. Ibid., 67.
12. Ibid., 40.
13. Ibid., 43, 44.
14. Ibid., 46.
15. Ibid., 71.
16. Ibid., 61.

Chapter Nine

The Chronicles of Narnia

Perhaps the most famous of Lewis's writings are the Chronicles of Narnia, seven books that take the reader into an imaginative land of exciting adventures and talking animals. These books are often classified separately from the rest of Lewis's fiction as books "for children." Yet even the casual reader can see that this is not an adequate description. While this series is certainly appropriate for children, Lewis did not limit it to a juvenile audience. On the contrary, he says that books that are truly appropriate for children to read are also worthy of adult readers. The sole exception to this, in Lewis's mind, are books of basic information.[1]

As an adult, Lewis continued to enjoy books that captured his imagination as a child. The Chronicles of Narnia include literary themes that captivated him throughout his life: adventure, quest, chivalry, magic, and mythology. Lewis wove these into stories that he would have enjoyed as a child and did enjoy as an adult. Consequently, they are appropriate for readers of all ages.

GENRE OF THE CHRONICLES

Like the rest of Lewis's fiction, the Chronicles of Narnia contain parallel meanings. For example, it is difficult to see the sacrificial death and resurrection of Aslan without seeing Christ. Yet here again, Lewis has avoided allegory in favor of a deeper form of poetic writing. In his essay "Sometimes Fairy Stories May Say Best What's to Be Said," Lewis explains his motivation for writing these stories. Drawing on his own childhood religious experience, he ponders the difficulty of having the proper feelings about God or the passion of Christ. He says a number of obstacles to these feelings. One obstacle occurs when faith was presented as an obligation. We should feel a certain way about these subjects, but this imperative command can actually squelch the true feeling. Another obstacle was the overly reverent way in which faith was presented. Is there a way to communicate these same truths while bypassing these and other obstacles? In this essay, Lewis describes his own strategy in the Chronicles of Narnia. If these vital Christian truths could be presented in a new manner—in an imaginary world—they might be viewed more objectively. The stumbling blocks of presentation might be avoided and the events themselves truly seen in their full power.[2]

Lest this seem too deliberate, Lewis clarifies himself in another essay, saying that the Chronicles of Narnia did not begin with a particular story but with an image. *The Lion, the Witch and the Wardrobe*, for example, began with an image of a Faun who is carrying an umbrella and an armful of packages through a snowy wood. Although Lewis had considered this image since his youth, it was only in his adulthood that he began to write a story about this picture. He says that as he wrote this story, he suddenly found Aslan appearing. This was apparently unintentional and derived from dreams about lions. Yet once this figure had become part of the story, Aslan became the focus of the series.[3] Understanding the genesis of these stories, it becomes evident that their primary purpose is simply to be stories—stories that are written for the joy of the narrative. While secondary meanings and parallels fill the books, these are not essential for enjoyment.

Aslan

Titles and Attributes

These secondary themes are, however, our chief interest. Most significant is Aslan, a talking lion and Christ figure. Lewis said that the name came from *Arabian Nights,* but he also noted a deliberate allusion to the Lion of Judah.[4] This allusion is intensified as Aslan is given other names, titles, and characteristics. Aslan is *the* Lion and is, therefore, called king, both of the wood and of the beasts. Indeed, he is above all kings, even above all High Kings (like Peter), yet Aslan is also the Son of the Emperor who is beyond the sea.[5] As king, Aslan is often called Lord, yet this lord is also truly a lion. When he confronts Bree, a talking horse who had doubted his existence, Aslan invites Bree to examine him closely. Touching and smelling Aslan, seeing his paws, tail, and whiskers, will convince Bree that Aslan truly is a lion. In this, Aslan parallels Jesus' words to Thomas (John 20:27). Because Aslan is to be the savior and lord of this world, he is as incarnate as those who populate it. He is, however, incarnate as the highest of beasts, the lion. Aslan is true beast, and truly the Son of the Emperor.[6]

Because of this, Aslan embodies a certain wildness. He is not a tame lion. This is frequently repeated in the Chronicles. He cannot be controlled by magic incantations or human contrivances. Aslan comes and goes as he pleases. "You can't keep him; it's not as if he were a *tame* lion."[7] His wildness is also cited by the wicked. In *The Last Battle*, those masquerading as Aslan and his entourage justify all manner of evil, saying that Aslan is not a tame lion. Sadly, even some who believed in Aslan fall victim to such statements. The last king of Narnia despairs over the apparent behavior of Aslan but notes that many tales declare that Aslan is not a tame lion.[8]

In other times, his creatures also know that Aslan is not tame, but they are well aware that he is good. His creatures cannot control him, but they can rely on his care.[9] Aslan is also patient. In *The Horse and His Boy*, Aslan guides Shasta throughout his entire life. When the boy finally notices the lion, he asks his identity. Aslan responds that he is one who has waited for Shasta's question for a long time. Time does not constrain Aslan because he is eternal. Some creatures use time to argue against the likelihood that Aslan will appear because too much time has passed. Even if Aslan were alive, he would be too old, something belied by Aslan's strength and vitality. In *The Last Battle*, Lewis again asserts Aslan's timelessness. Every world will end except for Aslan's country.[10]

Aslan is immutable. Each time he appears, no matter how much time has passed in Narnia or on Earth, Aslan is unchanged. Our understanding of him changes, however, because, as we mature, we know him better, so he seems bigger. Aslan is merciful, not showing himself to the Dufflepuds when they are not prepared to see him. He will not frighten them by openly revealing himself.[11] Finally, Aslan appears to be omniscient. Does Aslan know and fulfill a person's needs without being asked? He is aware of these needs, but he wants us to ask him for these things. Emeth, a righteous pagan, realizes that Aslan must be omniscient. Nor is his omniscience limited to Narnia. In *The Silver Chair*, Aslan knows everything that happened at an earthly school, and, at the end of the story, Aslan corrects it.[12] All these titles and attributes are a reflection of Aslan's identity.

ASLAN IS PROPHESIED

Although Aslan is active in Narnian history from beginning to end, not everyone sees this. There are stretches of time when creatures forget Aslan and his coming salvation. During such times, it is prophesied that at Aslan's coming wrongs will be righted, sorrow will disappear, and the seemingly endless season of winter will finally give way to spring.[13]

Aslan will bring justice, an end to sorrow, and springtime to Narnia's century of perpetual winter. A second prophesy notes that when Aslan fills the four thrones at Cair Paravel, the White Witch will lose not only her reign, but also her life. Aslan comes to bring the new life of spring and an end to the satanic figure.

ASLAN'S EFFECT ON PEOPLE

Aslan's identity is also seen in the effect that he has on people. The mention of his name is enough to cause a reaction. In *The Lion, the Witch and the Wardrobe,* the first children to enter Narnia do not know Aslan, but when he is described, each child responds according to his or her character.[14] Thus, the White Witch is enraged at the name of Aslan, threatening to kill anyone who speaks his name in her presence.

All types of creatures worship Aslan. Tree spirits bow to him as he passes. On board the *Dawn Treader*, a golden iconic image of Aslan hangs on the wall in Caspian's cabin, and the lion is depicted on the king's flag. People pray to him and praise him.[15] Aslan's name is used in a manner evocative of the trinitarian Invocation by creatures who cry, "Aslan, Aslan, Aslan." His followers use his name as a battle cry.[16] His prominence and significance are also seen when his name becomes an oath. Various people and animals swear by Aslan's name or by his mane.

Aslan is the object of faith. When Puddleglum's situation looks bleak, he reminds the children to heed and follow Aslan's words. His instructions are trustworthy. His word will always accomplish what he says it will do. This is true even if the solution is not what might have been expected. With Aslan, there are no accidents. Later, when a witch's spell enchants Puddleglum, Eustace, and Jill, the spell's power dissipates as the children are reminded of Aslan's existence. Their faith in Aslan is so strong that they confess that they will follow Aslan and his teachings even when someone tries to convince them that Aslan and Narnia do not exist.[17] This faith is manifested as critical actions are completed in Aslan's name, such as freeing a captive prince and a covert invasion of enemy territory in time of battle.[18]

ASLAN IS KNOWN BY HIS WORK

Above all, Aslan's identity is revealed through his actions. Aslan calls people to come to him. In *The Silver Chair*, the children think they have entered Narnia at their own request, but Aslan says, "You would not have called to me unless I had been calling to you."[19] Despite all this, people are not always glad to see Aslan. At times he comes in judgment, to chastise. When Lucy blames others for not following Aslan, he silences her with a growl. When Edmund and Caspian argue over the ownership of a spring that transforms everything to gold, Aslan walks past, silencing them with his presence.[20] But Aslan also forgives, demonstrating this with his presence and love.[21]

Aslan strengthens his people. Strength flows from his mane and is carried on his breath. For example, when Lucy lacked courage, she tried to hide her face in Aslan's mane. Instead of concealing her, she found that Aslan's strength entered her. Aslan breathes on Susan so she can forget her fears; when he breathes on Edmund, Edmund appears more great and noble than before. Aslan parallels Christ's post-resurrection appearances when he proves he is not a ghost by breathing on Shasta. Aslan shows mercy to the wicked Telmarines, who are pirates from Earth. When he sends them back, Aslan breathes on one, bringing a new look into the man's eyes. Aslan bestows himself, his nature, and his comfort through his breath and mane.[22]

Aslan's gift of strength is seen in *The Voyage of the Dawn Treader* when the ship is shrouded in darkness in a place of nightmares. Amid their despair, light shines on the ship. At the center of the light is an object that looks at first like a cross, then like an airplane, then a kite, and finally an albatross. The albatross circles the mast three times and calls out in a voice no one understands. When it speaks to Lucy, calling her to have courage, she recognizes the voice as Aslan's. With the voice, there comes a delicious smell.[23] There is an interesting blending of images in this passage that reveals Lewis's conception of Aslan. The albatross parallels the Holy Spirit, but the voice is Aslan's. The albatross circles the mast three times, suggestive of the Trinity. It enlightens the people and shows them the way. While this may introduce confusion as to the nature of the Trinity, it does stress Aslan's role.

There is one more type of passage to consider. At times, Aslan strengthens the faithful people by terrifying their enemies. Therefore, time and time again, the lion roars to scare away the White Witch, soldiers, evil creatures, or bad schoolchildren. Aslan will do everything to comfort his people. All these actions demonstrate that Aslan embodies a divine role.

ASLAN CREATES NARNIA

Aslan is further revealed at the creation of Narnia. A group of humans arrives in Narnia and find it empty and dark. In this void, beautiful, wordless singing begins, seeming to come simultaneously from all directions. That singular voice is suddenly joined by countless others, singing in harmony. Following this, the stars appear. It seemed to those watching that it was the first voice that made the stars appear and, in response, the stars themselves began to sing. Most enjoy the sound of the music, except for an evil magician and Jadis, who will become the White Witch of Narnia. The singer is Aslan, and his appearance eclipses everything else. As the music progresses and changes, effects are seen in the creation. One of the children perceived that all the things that were being created came from the lion's head. He is in control of creation.[24]

The song changes again, and the earth bubbles up, bursting to reveal animals. Aslan separates a pair of each of the animals and breathes on them. Then, in a flash of light that emanated either from Aslan or from the sky, Aslan calls Narnia to awake. The separated animals begin to speak. Not all are given the gift of speech, only the pair that was separated from the others. Aslan creates both the speaking and mute animals.[25] Elsewhere in the Chronicles, Peter affirms that Aslan created all things and gave the gift of speech to certain animals.[26]

ASLAN EXERCISES PROVIDENCE

Aslan not only creates Narnia, he continues to care for it through his providence. He provides for his creatures, keeps watch over them, controls their lives, and is supreme over all other gods and over nature. He satisfies the hungry in *The Lion, the Witch and the Wardrobe* when, following a great battle, a meal is miraculously provided for all who are present. In *The Last Battle*, a group of dwarfs is fed a wonderful banquet, though they do not see it, believing, instead, that they are eating straw. Also in *The Last Battle*, Tirian and those with him become thirsty in the midst of battle. They are refreshed from a spring of water that flows from a rock. This parallels Moses and the rock that provided water during the wandering of the Israelites in the desert after the Exodus. In 1 Corinthians 10:4, we note that this rock is a type of Christ.[27]

Aslan provides for his people who travel to the end of the earth to see him. There, on the last bit of land, is found "Aslan's Table," a remarkable feast that is miraculously replenished each day for the nourishment and enjoyment of travelers.[28] Aslan also providentially watches over his people. In *Prince Caspian*, while celebrators sleep, Aslan remains awake, keeping watch. If it is necessary for some to face danger, Aslan makes the situation tolerable. When leopards are sent as messengers to the White Witch (who has the power to turn them into stone), the children know that Aslan would not send the leopards if all were not right. When Eustace falls off a great cliff in *The Silver Chair*, Aslan rushes to the site and blows him to safety. Although this complicates Aslan's plan, he does it to protect Eustace from injury or death.[29]

Another demonstration of providence is the story of Shasta in *The Horse and His Boy*. Here an entire life is interpreted from the omniscient perspective of Aslan. Many different events were directly controlled by Aslan. From infancy, the lion had protected and guided Shasta. Aslan's care encompasses aspects of Shasta's life of which he was unaware. All things had been done for his good and his safety, even those things that seemed at the time to be ordinary or even detrimental.[30]

Finally, the extent of Aslan's authority is seen in his control of nature and of nature-gods. In *Prince Caspian*, Aslan wakes the tree spirits as he woke them at the beginning of creation; the trees and gods (such as Bacchus, Silenus, and Bromius) do his bidding. Aslan also makes it safe for humans to be near these gods. The children remark that they would not like to meet them without Aslan. Aslan even works mediately through Bacchus. Whereas Jesus at the wedding of Cana turned water into wine miraculously, Aslan does the same through this pagan god.[31]

Aslan works mediately. That is, rather than becoming directly involved, he works through intermediates. Aslan appoints good governments (bad governments arise spontaneously). He establishes thrones and rulers, making Peter first a knight and then High King, titles Peter receives only at Aslan's will.[32] Aslan works among his people, giving the chief gift of freedom. He frees Edmund from death and Eustace from his dragon state. He frees a river god from a bridge, students from a bad teacher, and a teacher from her bad students. An old woman, the former nurse of King Caspian, is delivered from her illness. In these and many other ways, Aslan brings freedom to Narnia, but the true freedom is the freedom from death that is experienced by his faithful followers.[33]

ASLAN DESTROYS NARNIA

Because Aslan created Narnia, it is he who calls for the end of the world and brings it to pass at his command. Indeed, only his heavenly world will endure forever. All other worlds will end. The final judgment and destruction of Narnia is found in *The Last Battle*. Narnia is afflicted with tribulation, unbelief, and apostasy, though a faithful remnant exists when Aslan returns to judge all creatures. Some pass to the left of Aslan and disappear in his shadow, never to be seen again by the blessed. The other beasts look at Aslan and love him, though many of them are afraid. These enter a door at Aslan's right, thereby entering the Real Narnia and Aslan's country. Following this, dragons and great lizards devour Narnia, much as described in the Ragnarok of Norse mythology, a favorite mythology of the young Lewis. Once the destruction is complete, Narnia is left in frozen darkness. As High King, Peter is ordered by Aslan to shut and lock the door.[34]

ASLAN IS DIRECTLY REVEALED

One particularly clear revelation of Aslan occurs at the end of *The Voyage of the Dawn Treader*. The *Dawn Treader* has sailed close to the end of the world where lilies cover the sea. The three children from Earth leave the *Dawn Treader* in a small boat, drifting eastward. After three days, they reach land and, getting out, see a lamb that is so white they can barely look at it. The lamb invites them to eat a breakfast of fish. The parallels to Christ are clear. The children travel for the same number of days Jesus was in the tomb. They pass through a sea of lilies—a common Easter symbol. They are served a meal of fish beside the sea just as Jesus fed His disciples after the resurrection (John 21:9–12). The lamb then speaks, telling the children that his country can be reached from all worlds, including our own. While he is speaking, the lamb is transformed until the children see that it is really Aslan.[35]

Aslan appears to them in the form of two Christological symbols—the lion and the lamb—to tell the children that they are returning home but that they will be able to get into his heavenly country from their world. Aslan then promises that he will continually tell them how to get to his world. He does not reveal all the details, however. The children are told that Aslan's world lies over a river, but they are not told whether the journey is long or short. They are not told all the specifics, but they are given everything they need to know. Aslan will be with them.[36] Edmund asks Aslan if he is present in our world as well. Aslan tells him that he is here also, then continues:

> I have another name. You must learn to know me by that name. This was the very reason why you were brought to Narnia, that by knowing me here for a little, you may know me better there.[37]

Here is a clear explanation and a connection between Narnia and Earth, between Aslan and Christ. The last words of Aslan are written to the reader of the Chronicles as well: The reason you have been brought to this world is so you might know me better in your own. Aslan's identity is obvious and becomes even more so as his work is considered.

Aslan Redeems

At the heart of the Chronicles of Narnia is the vicarious death of Aslan. Edmund, one of four children to enter Narnia, meets the White Witch, who holds Narnia under a spell of winter. The witch knows that if the children become the kings and queens of Narnia, her reign will end and she will die. Intending to kill the children, she persuades Edmund to betray his brother and sisters. When this plan fails, she decides to kill Edmund, but he is rescued first. This deliverance, however, is insufficient because the witch still holds claim on Edmund's life. The witch reminds Aslan that she has a right to his blood because the penalty for treachery and betrayal is death. Consequently, she considers Edmund's life and his blood to be her property. If this price is not paid, she claims that Narnia will be destroyed by fire and water. Aslan agrees with her words. This is a correct summary of the Emperor's Law.[38]

The law that condemns Edmund to death for betraying his brother and sisters to the evil one is not the invention of the witch. On the contrary, this is the "deep magic" written on the stone table of sacrifice and engraved on the scepter of the emperor. Because this is the emperor's magic, it cannot be ignored. Instead, Aslan makes a secret deal with the witch, trading his life for Edmund's.

That evening, Aslan walks slowly to the stone table where the witch waits, surrounded by monsters from a child's nightmare. He is willingly bound, shaved, ridiculed, muzzled, kicked, hit, spat on, and mocked. Finally, the witch tells him he has failed and kills him with a stone knife. Afterward, Susan and Lucy clean and care for Aslan's body. At dawn, they hear the table crack in two and find that Aslan's body is missing. He appears before them, proving with his breath and his roar that he is alive. Then he explains what has happened. The witch knew the law from the beginning of time, namely, that sin's penalty must be paid. That is the "deep magic," yet there is a "deeper magic" from before time that she did not know: If an innocent victim should be killed on the stone table, it will break and death will work backward.[39] That is precisely what has happened. Aslan was an innocent victim, and an innocent victim killed for another could not remain dead. He rose according to the deeper magic. Because of his death, Edmund's treachery is forgiven and his life spared.

If *The Lion, the Witch and the Wardrobe* were the only book written, it might appear that Aslan died only for Edmund. In the context of all seven books, however, the benefits of Aslan's death are applied to others. For example, after Aslan is brought back to life, the first thing he does is go to the witch's castle. There, by breathing on the creatures the witch has turned into statues, Aslan frees them. The former statues think they have been asleep and are reunited with friends. While the parallel to the resurrection of the dead is obvious, this is not the final resurrection (which is presented in *The Last Battle*). In *The Lion, the Witch and the Wardrobe*, the statues are brought back to life and join the fight against the witch. In that battle, Edmund breaks the witch's magic wand and hampers her progress, but it is Aslan who kills her. The battle complete, celebration ensues and peace prevails in Narnia.[40]

This is the chief description of salvation in the Chronicles, but it is not the sole image. Another application is seen in Edmund's cousin, Eustace. After being troublesome for the entire journey on the *Dawn Treader*, Eustace stumbles upon a dragon's lair. There he witnesses the dragon's death and claims the creature's treasure hoard as his own. Lying on the treasure, thinking dragon thoughts, Eustace becomes a dragon. In time, Eustace repents, yet no one can find a way to help him. His salvation has to come from Aslan.

One night a lion comes to Eustace and leads him to a mountaintop garden. In the center of the garden (which is actually in "Aslan's country") is a well. Eustace wants to bathe in this well, but he is told he must undress first. He begins to remove his skin. After removing three layers of dragon skin, Eustace sees that he is still a dragon. The lion takes over, tearing deep into his skin; indeed, the lion tears all the way down to Eustace's heart. Then the lion picks him up and throws him into the water. Eustace emerges as a boy again.[41]

After this event, Eustace still does not know the identity of the lion, so Edmund tells him about Aslan: "He knows me. ... He is the great Lion, the son of the Emperor over the Sea who saved me and saved Narnia."[42] Edmund's words are crucial here. Aslan saves not only Edmund, but he saves Narnia as well. Although

Edmund's betrayal had caused Aslan's death, all of Narnia benefits. Aslan has saved Eustace through an act suggestive of Baptism. Eustace's old dragon-self is destroyed, and a new person emerges from the water. Lewis is careful to note that though Eustace began acting like a different boy, he still had relapses into his old ways.[43] However, Eustace was improving because Aslan has changed him.

Another application of Aslan's work occurs at the end of *The Silver Chair*. Following the death of King Caspian, the children are taken to the "Mountain of Aslan," which is beyond the end of the world. There, Caspian lies dead in a stream, water flowing over him. Eustace, Jill, and even Aslan wept at the sight. Then something remarkable happens. Aslan asks Eustace to get a long, sharp thorn. He makes Eustace drive the thorn into his paw. A large drop of blood drips into the stream over the corpse of Caspian. His body begins to change until he rises from the water and stands before them, young again.[44]

As Caspian runs to embrace Aslan, the children are puzzled. Had not Caspian died? Aslan answers, "He has died. Most people have … . Even I have."[45] By the blood of Aslan, another soul is saved, the body raised to eternal life. The salvation won by Aslan for Edmund is applied to others.

There is one more aspect of Aslan's death to consider. After his death, the stone table and knife used to kill him are treated as relics. Many years after Aslan's death, the place where Aslan was slain is altered so the site is enclosed within the hill. It is known as Aslan's How. Inside are tunnels, passages, and chambers adorned with the figure of the lion. Deep in the heart of this hill, the children discover a secret chamber that contains the stone table upon which Aslan was slain. It has been split down the center and the ancient writing once inscribed on its sides has nearly vanished.[46] The stone table has been enshrined, set apart from the rest of the world. Aslan's How is the closest thing to a shrine in all of Narnia, and it is focused upon the place of sacrifice. The stone knife is also treated as a relic. After its use for Aslan's death, its next appearance is on Aslan's table at the end of the world. There it would be held in honor until the end of the world.

A crucial element in the identity and nature of Aslan remains. Lewis inserts several clues to the full identity of Aslan. One clue already studied is the revelation to the children at the end of *The Voyage of the Dawn Treader*. In this revelation, Aslan appears as a lamb, then as the lion, and finally in another form (presumably human). Other direct indications are also present. Aslan and Father Christmas come at the same time. Similarly, in *The Last Battle*, the followers of Aslan are forced into a stable. They believe they are going to their death. To their surprise, when they enter the stable, they find Aslan's country, an enormous world that is far larger than the stable. Lucy is not surprised at all. She responds, "In our world too, a Stable once had something inside it that was bigger than our whole world."[47]

In *The Voyage of the Dawn Treader*, Lucy discovers a book of spells. While one of the spells enables her to eavesdrop on a classmate, which causes Lucy to grow angry, another spell brings Lucy a sense of peace. This is a spell designed to refresh one's spirit. It is adorned with beautiful pictures and is written on three pages. Lucy describes it as a lovely story, and though she later cannot recall all the details, she knows some of the story's features, including a cup, a sword, a tree, and a green hill. All these elements figure prominently in the Gospel accounts of our Lord's passion. Furthermore, in a marvelous explanation of the Gospel story, as Lucy reads the spells, Aslan is made visible. When Lucy wants to hear the story repeated, Aslan assures her that he will tell her the story for years to come.[48]

A final issue is the relationship between Aslan and the Trinity. This is a particularly difficult problem that is made more so by the primary audience for these books—children. Lewis is keeping things simple, yet an interaction of the Trinity is seen in Aslan. The first hint of this is in the incantations people use to summon Aslan's help. Both beasts and people repeatedly call out Aslan's name not once but three times. Aslan is the only way to approach God. There is no direct appeal to the Emperor-over-the-Sea without Aslan. Aslan's name serves as the name for the entire godhead.[49] There is also the case of the *Dawn Treader* in the darkness of nightmares where Aslan seems present as the Holy Spirit. Third, Aslan's role in creation is much broader and more inclusive than the role normally ascribed to Christ. In a unique passage in *The Horse and His Boy*, Shasta finds himself accompanied in a blinding fog by a lion. He asks the lion's identity, and Aslan responds:

> "Myself," said the Voice, very deep and low so that the earth shook: and again "Myself," loud and clear and gay: and then the third time "Myself," whispered so softly you

could hardly hear it, and yet it seemed to come from all round you as if the leaves rustled with it.[50]

This is the closest thing to an explicit revelation of the Trinity to be found in the Chronicles. The first voice, shaking the earth, is the voice of creation, the Father. The second is loud, clear, and gay, the voice of the one who stands beside Shasta, who speaks with organic means. The third soft, mysterious voice is that of the Holy Spirit, whom Lewis primarily considered as God in us. Taken by itself, this passage is not an adequate presentation of the Trinity, but it should not be read in isolation. These novels are not statements of propositional theology, but they are illustrations. Here we see that Aslan is God, active among his creatures as the Second Person of the Trinity, but he does not act alone.

THE ATONEMENT

In avoiding any one theory of the atonement, Lewis drew from as many sources as possible. Yet in reading the Chronicles, one does see a particular model being expressed. While it may seem, at first, to be the *Christus Victor* model, it is, in reality, a subpart of that model, the ransom theory. The identification of this theory should not be interpreted to mean that Lewis did not use elements of other theories. Writing in the *Scottish Journal of Theology*, Charles A. Taliaferro notes how the ransom theory finds expression in Narnia.[51] Somehow (the method is not explained to the reader), an evildoer comes to be in captivity to Satan, that is, to the White Witch. The Savior gives himself in place of the evildoer. As a result, and unforeseen by the witch, she is overthrown. This sense of overthrow is what makes the event seem like an expression of the *Christus Victor* theory.

While the Chronicles make use of elements of other atonement models, including the Anselmic theory (recall that the emperor's "magic" cannot be overthrown), there is no usage of the Abelardian model, which sees Christ merely as an example. This falls short of Lewis's understanding. If Lewis has a model of the atonement at all, it is an eclectic one. He takes elements from each theory as they best suit his purpose of presenting Christ.

CONCLUSION

So who is Aslan? Is he equivalent to Christ? The answer must be no. Aslan was not created to replace Christ or to explain Christ on a point-by-point basis, but he is typical of Christ. How might the story of Christ appear if a world of talking animals, a world like Narnia, really did exist? What would Christ be like if He were incarnate so He could redeem that world? It is a hypothetical situation, and Aslan is only a fictional answer to that question, but the situation is real. Narnia is imagined, but the incarnation and redemption are historical fact. Christ has truly done these things in our world.[52]

Because of this, Aslan cannot replace Christ. This is illustrated in a series of letters that C. S. Lewis wrote to children. When one child wrote to ask about Aslan's name in our world, Lewis responded that he wanted the child to figure it out. But then he gave the child some clues. Aslan arrived at Christmastime. He was the son of a great emperor. Aslan died for another person and returned to life again. Finally, Aslan is a lion who also calls himself a lamb. Lewis does not complete the connection for this child, but he simply asks if the child can't figure out Aslan's name on Earth.[53]

Even more revealing is a letter Lewis wrote to a worried parent on May 6, 1955. This mother was troubled that her son loved Aslan more than he loved Jesus. Lewis comforted her, saying that this really is not possible. All the things that this boy loved in Aslan were really things that were done and said by Jesus. The boy was confused by the names, but the facts were the same.[54]

These images are present in the Chronicles. Lewis acknowledged them to be present, and he helped guide people to discover them. In Aslan, Lewis has successfully "translated" Christ to his readers. Lewis presents Christ's redemption in a new form so it might be understood by many people. This is also the primary meaning of the story. Yet in a myth of this scale, additional layers of meaning must be present. It is obvious that Aslan is a type of Christ and that Lewis points his readers to Christ. Consistent with Lewis's intent, the reader may see the person, work, and atonement of Aslan and there recognize an action similar to that undertaken by the Savior of the world.

NOTES

1. C. S. Lewis, "On Stories," in *On Stories and Other Essays on Literature* (New York: Harcourt Brace Jovanovich, 1982), 14.

2. C. S. Lewis, "Sometimes Fairy Stories May Say Best What's to Be Said," in *On Stories and Other Essays on Literature*, 47.

3. C. S. Lewis, "It All Began with a Picture," in *On Stories and Other Essays on Literature*, 53.

4. Lyle W. Dorsett and Marjorie Lamp Mead eds., *C. S. Lewis Letters to Children* (New York, MacMillan, 1985), 29.

5. C. S. Lewis, *The Lion, the Witch and the Wardrobe* (New York: MacMillan, 1950), 74, 75; and C. S. Lewis, *Prince Caspian* (New York: MacMillan, 1951), 39, 202.

6. C. S. Lewis, *The Silver Chair* (New York: MacMillan, 1953), 187; and C. S. Lewis, *The Horse and His Boy* (New York: MacMillan, 1954), 193.

7. C. S. Lewis, *The Voyage of the Dawn Treader* (New York: MacMillan, 1952), 138.

8. C. S. Lewis, *The Last Battle* (New York: MacMillan, 1956), 16.

9. Lewis, *Lion*, 76.

10. Lewis, *Horse and His Boy*, 157; Lewis, *Dawn Treader*, 138; and Lewis, *Last Battle*, 89.

11. Lewis, *Caspian*, 136; and Lewis, *Dawn Treader*, 138.

12. C. S. Lewis, *The Magician's Nephew* (New York, MacMillan, 1955), 150; Lewis, *Last Battle*, 165; and Lewis, *Silver Chair*, 214.

13. Lewis, *Lion*, 74, 75.

14. Ibid., 64, 65.

15. Lewis, *Caspian*, 138, 139; and Lewis, *Dawn Treader*, 13, 46, 159.

16. Lewis, *Silver Chair*, 7; and Lewis, *Caspian*, 190.

17. Lewis, *Silver Chair*, 104, 134, 156, 159.

18. Lewis, *Silver Chair*, 146; and Lewis, *Last Battle*, 58.

19. Lewis, *Silver Chair*, 19.

20. Lewis, *Caspian*, 136; and Lewis, *Dawn Treader*, 108.

21. Lewis, *Lion*, 136.

22. Lewis, *Caspian*, 138, 148, 174; Lewis, *Horse and His Boy*, 157; and Lewis, *Caspian*, 213.

23 Lewis, *Dawn Treader*, 159, 160.

24. Lewis, *Magician's Nephew*, 98, 99, 107.

25. Ibid., 116.

26. The entire creation account is found in Lewis, *Magician's Nephew*, 98–119; and Lewis, *Last Battle*, 134.

27. Lewis, *Lion*, 178; and Lewis, *Last Battle*, 128.

28. Lewis, *Dawn Treader*, 165, 166.

29. Lewis, *Caspian*, 207; Lewis, *Lion*, 137; and Lewis, *Silver Chair*, 13.

30. Lewis, *Horse and His Boy*, 158.

31. Lewis, *Caspian*, 184, 152, 154.

32. Lewis, *Lion*, 126; and Lewis, *Caspian*, 172, 200.

33. Lewis, *Caspian*, 193, 194, 196, 197.

34. Lewis, *Last Battle*, 150–57.

35. Lewis, *Dawn Treader*, 215.

36. Ibid.

37. Ibid., 216.

38. Lewis, *Lion*, 139.

39. Ibid., 160.

40. Ibid., 165ff.; especially, 167, 168, 174.

41. Lewis, *Dawn Treader*, 88–91.

42. Ibid., 92.

43. Ibid., 93.

44. Lewis, *Silver Chair*, 212, 213.

45. Ibid., 213.

46. Lewis, *Caspian*, 86, 89.

47. Lewis, *Last Battle*, 140, 141.

48. Lewis, *Dawn Treader*, 133, 135, 136.

49. Lewis, *Silver Chair*, 7.

50. Lewis, *Horse and His Boy*, 159.

51. Charles A. Taliaferro, "A Narnian Theory of the Atonement," *Scottish Journal of Theology* 41.1 (1988): 75–92, 79.

52. W. H. Lewis, ed. *The Letters of C. S. Lewis* (New York: Harcourt, Brace, Jovanovich, 1966), 261, 283.

53. Dorsett and Mead, *Letters to Children*, 32.

54. Ibid., 52.

Chapter Ten

Till We Have Faces

Till We Have Faces is the last novel C. S. Lewis wrote. In many ways, it is the culmination of a lifetime of work. It retells the intriguing myth of Cupid and Psyche, which had long fascinated Lewis. He began experimenting with the myth while he was a student, twice attempting to tell it in poetic verse before abandoning his efforts. More than 30 years after his first attempt, Lewis returned to the myth in earnest.

The myth tells of Cupid's love for a human woman named Psyche. Because Cupid is a god of love, and Psyche is the Greek word meaning "soul," it is easy to see the original myth as an allegory of the relationship between humans and the gods. Lewis recasts the narrative to convey new and deeper themes. In the introduction to the British edition of *Till We Have Faces*, he says the themes include a straight tale of barbarism, the mind of an ugly woman, the tension between idolatry and enlightenment, and the effect of faith or a vocation on a human life.[1] Through all of this runs the deep theme of love. In *The Four Loves*, Lewis discusses various types of love. Here he demonstrates them in a fictional context. As God's love is revealed to us through Christ, this novel presents christological themes.

Till We Have Faces is set in the kingdom of Glome, which is ruled by the tyrannical King Throm. Throm has two daughters, Orual and Redival. In time, a third daughter, Istra (or Psyche), is born. Psyche grows into a beautiful and compassionate child. It is not long before people begin to worship her and to come to her for healing and food. This causes Psyche to fall under the wrath of Ungit, a fertility goddess. Because of Ungit's jealousy, Psyche becomes "The Accursed," and Glome is afflicted with plagues and sufferings. These stop after Psyche is sacrificed to Ungit's son in the "Great Offering."

Following the sacrifice, Orual returns to the place of sacrifice to bury Psyche, but she finds her alive. Psyche claims to be married to a god, but she has never seen her husband in the light. She tells her sister that she lives in a palace, but Orual cannot see her home. Fearing that Psyche is being exploited, Orual convinces her to examine her husband in the light, something he has forbidden her to do. When Psyche looks on her divine husband, the palace is destroyed. Psyche is banished and sent to accomplish impossible tasks. Orual now sees the beautiful god and is horrified by her actions. The god judges her, tells her what has happened to Psyche, and cryptically proclaims that Orual, too, will be Psyche. Orual hears these words as a judgment against her.

Later, Orual ascends to the throne of Glome. After some prosperous but sad years as queen, she travels to other lands. At the farthest reach of her journey, Orual discovers a temple to the new goddess, Istra. She hears the story of Psyche, but the details are wrong. In response, Orual writes her own account as a complaint against the gods. When her case is heard by the gods, Orual sees that her complaint is filled with cruel, self-centered words that have no merit of their own. In the end, Orual, who had been jealous and ugly, is brought a vessel of beauty and becomes as lovely as Psyche. She ends the book with a recognition that the gods were correct all along and that she was in error. Before she completes the last words, she dies.

That is a skeletal overview of the book, which is filled with deeper meanings. There are many significant themes within the narrative as Lewis reveals his understanding of sin, pagan worship, philosophy, and modernizing tendencies in religion. Lewis also develops themes that reflect his Christological understanding.

PSYCHE AS CHRIST

The most Christlike person in this narrative is Psyche. From the beginning, it is clear that she is not a normal child. She is beautiful, and everything she touches becomes beautiful. She dreams of the mountain where the god dwells, creating stories about it that foreshadow her later life. Psyche imagines that she will be a great queen, the wife of the greatest of all kings. The king will build her a glorious castle, made of gold and amber, on top of the god's mountain.[2] As she grows older, clear parallels to Christ emerge. People begin to venerate Psyche, seeking healing and food, but later they reject her. Orual says, "You healed them, and blessed them, and took their filthy disease upon yourself. And these are their thanks."[3]

The most significant themes are found as Psyche is offered as a sacrifice for Glome. The priest of Ungit explains how the Great Offering responds to the plagues afflicting the nation. In the past, he said, a man had lain with his sister and killed the child. Once they discovered his identify, they "expiated" his sin, and all was right.[4] Another time, a woman cursed Ungit's son, and floods covered the land. When they "expiated" her sin, the river receded. Whenever such disasters occur, there is "an Accursed" who must die for his or her sin. The Great Offering, however, requires a perfect victim. This contradiction confuses the king. How can the victim be the Accursed but also be perfect? The priest is not disturbed by this paradox, seeing no reason why the Accursed could not simultaneously be the best and the worst.

According to the custom, lots are cast to identify the Accursed. They point to Psyche. Although the king is not pleased that his daughter will die, he is relieved that he will not be the victim. He begins to justify the situation, arguing that one person often dies to save others. It is a common occurrence in warfare.[5] When Psyche is confined to await her sacrifice, Orual goes to comfort Psyche and is comforted in return.[6] Psyche knows that she will be sacrificed, and she realizes the significance of this. She understands that she must be the Accursed and that her death is necessary. She cannot be a ransom for the entire nation unless she dies, and this is the only way that she, a mortal, can go to be with the god.[7] In the same way, our Lord knew that His death was necessary to accomplish the salvation of the world.

The Great Offering is made on top of a mountain where the god lives. Psyche is taken up, chained to a tree, and left to die. Here, Lewis has made a particularly significant change. In the original myth, the victim was sacrificed on a rock. In *Till We Have*

Faces, by contrast, Psyche is left to die on a tree just as Christ was killed on Calvary's tree. And as Christ willingly went to His death, so does Psyche go willingly to her fate. She went to her death bravely and stoically. She gave no emotional display nor did she cry out. Courageously and patiently, Psyche accepted her fate.[8] Psyche submits to the sacrifice for Glome, evoking thoughts of Isaiah's prophecy of Christ: "He was oppressed and afflicted, yet He did not open His mouth; He was led like a lamb to the slaughter, and as a sheep before her shearers is silent, so He did not open His mouth" (Isaiah 53:7).

As Christ's sacrifice accomplished what God intended, so Psyche's sacrifice was effective. At her death, the plagues ended and, almost immediately, rain began to fall.[9] Afterward, Psyche is called "the Blessed"—the precise opposite of her name during the Great Offering. Orual travels to the place of her death, but instead of a body, she sees the living Psyche. Psyche has been given a kingdom that cannot be seen by mortal eyes. Her house lies across a river, a symbol of death. Momentarily, Orual glimpses the house, but only when she kneels by a river, an action evocative of Baptism.[10] Likewise, Christ lives after His crucifixion. His followers who went to His grave found it empty. He has received a heavenly kingdom, and His "palace" lies beyond our death.

In Orual's last vision before the gods, she sees that Psyche must get a casket of beauty from death and bring it back to Ungit. Many try to deter her, but Psyche goes anyway. When she returns from this descent into hell, she gives the beauty to Orual, who now becomes Psyche. As Christ descended into hell and returned to give His riches to His people, so Psyche returns from the land of the dead and shares her "victory" with Orual.

With all of these parallels, it is tempting to make Psyche an allegorical Christ, yet in a letter written to Clyde Kilby, Lewis indicated otherwise. He told Dr. Kilby that Psyche could be described as an *"anima naturaliter Christiana,"* or "a natural Christian soul." She was part of a pagan religion, but she made the best of her situation. By participating in the parts of this religion that were true, Psyche was being guided, at least in a vague way, toward the one true God. This explains the Christian parallels. It is only natural that Psyche is like Christ because, in some way, every good person is like Christ.[11]

Lewis indicates that *Till We Have Faces* is not an allegory but a myth. Psyche is not Christ, but she is like Christ. Indeed, she must be like Christ because she is good, and all goodness conforms to His image. Psyche is not Christ, just as Aslan is not Christ and Ransom is not Christ. But Psyche does exemplify characteristics and behavior that may broaden one's understanding of Christ. It may be that Lewis did not intend Psyche to be such a strong Christ figure. Yet even if unintentional, the parallels exist. While not a perfect allegorical figure, Psyche exemplifies numerous Christological features.

IMAGES OF THE TRUE GOD

In this book, as in Lewis's other works, there are obvious indications of Lewis's Christianity. For example, when Orual despairs and considers suicide, a god warns her that one cannot escape Ungit in death. The grim goddess is just as present in death as she is on earth. Instead, Orual is advised to die before she dies.[12] While unexplained here, this advice indicates the need for spiritual regeneration. This is heightened by the god's warning that there is no opportunity to do this after one has physically died.

Another notable Christian parallel is seen in the words of Bardia, who questions whether the gods can know what the human experience is truly like. Can they relate to human feelings?[13] The plea of a human being for God's understanding is answered in Christ's incarnation. God does indeed know what it feels like to be a man because God has taken on human flesh.

Finally, there is a marvelous passage on divine justice in which Orual questions the Fox about whether the gods are just. He responds, "Oh no, child. What would become of us if they were?"[14] This reinforces Lewis's continual emphasis that it is much better to receive divine mercy than justice.

CONCLUSION

Till We Have Faces offers much less Christological material than the rest of Lewis's fiction. It does, however, provide an intriguing Christ figure. While Psyche is not Christ, she does reflect His work. Her substitutionary death and continuing life are a reflection of the vicarious passion of Christ, who Himself might have said, "How can I be the offering unless I die?" Like Psyche, Christ in His crucifixion is both the Blessed and the Accursed. As the kingdom of Glome received rain after the sacrifice of Psyche, and as Orual received beauty when Psyche returned from the Underworld, so humanity receives the fruits of Christ's death and resurrection: the forgiveness of sins and everlasting life.

NOTES

1. C. S. Lewis, *Till We Have Faces* (London: Geoffrey Bles, 1956), 1.
2. C. S. Lewis, *Till We Have Faces* (San Diego: Harcourt, Brace, Jovanovich, 1958), 23.
3. Ibid., 28, 31, 39.
4. Ibid., 46.
5. Ibid., 49, 50, 61; cf. John 11:49–50.
6. Ibid., 67.
7. Ibid., 72.
8. Ibid., 85
9. Ibid., 83, 84.
10. Ibid., 90, 95, 116, 133.
11. W. H. Lewis, ed. *The Letters of C. S. Lewis* (New York: Harcourt, Brace, Jovanovich, 1966), 274.
12. Lewis, *Till We Have Faces*, 279.
13. Ibid., 66.
14. Ibid., 297.

Chapter Eleven

Devotional Writings

C. S. Lewis published his first Christian work less than two years after his conversion. He continued publishing for the rest of his life. His developing faith and understanding is reflected in his writings. While he wrote books with Christian themes for 30 years, in the last five years of his life, he returned to writing explicitly theological works. Like his earlier apologetic works, these books directly present Christian teaching, but they are not intended to defend the Christian faith. They are less forceful and more candid and conversational in tone. Lewis addresses them to Christians and intends them to be used for edification. For this reason, these books might best be classified as "devotional writings." Lewis indicates as much in the opening pages of *Reflections on the Psalms*. He notes that, unlike his earlier books, this is not a work of apologetics. It is not written to demonstrate the truth of Christianity to unbelievers. To the contrary, he writes to Christians, or at least to those who are willing to read this book from the perspective of a believer. He explains that this is necessary because there is an essential difference between defending the truth and feeding upon it,[1] and both of these activities are necessary.

These devotional writings provide a glimpse into the Christian thinking of the mature Lewis and show a different facet of his theological thought. They will be addressed in the order of their publication.

REFLECTIONS ON THE PSALMS

In *Reflections on the Psalms*, Lewis combines his Christian faith and his professional literary skills. However, he begins the book by noting his weaknesses. He admits that it is not a scholarly work and that he is not an expert in its content. As a layman, he intends to write for other laymen and asks that they recognize his limitations.[2] This disclaimer is partially correct. Lewis did not have theological training, and because he did not know Hebrew, he worked with the Psalms only in translation. At the same time, he was well acquainted with the Psalter. His daily attendance at his college chapel with its regular reading of the Psalms led to an intimate familiarity with their content. Furthermore, Lewis was a poet, and, as he reminds the reader, the Psalms must be read as poetry to be fully understood. Reading them as poetry, Lewis sees many themes, including Christological themes. He writes of the incarnation, of different ways of understanding Christ, and of Christ types outside of Scripture. Lewis may have approached the Psalter as an amateur, but he produced a significant exposition of the Psalms. In fact, his work was so well respected that, soon after its publication, Lewis was invited to work on a revised version of the Psalms for use in the Church of England.

THE INCARNATION

As Lewis discusses the Psalms, some significant facets of his Christology emerge. For example, as he discusses what it means for the Psalms to be the Word of God, he alludes to the Athanasian Creed's description of Christ's incarnation. This creed says that the incarnation is not "conversion of the Godhead into flesh but ... taking the manhood into God." Lewis summarizes this, saying that in the incarnation, human life bears divine life.[3] Likewise, the Word of God was not converted into literature, but literature was taken up to bear God's Word. While he is trying to explain inspiration, note his Christological doctrine. Quoting from the Athanasian Creed, Lewis simply says that this is something we are taught. He is within the bounds of orthodoxy because he has merely restated the creedal formulation.

Lewis shows more creativity as he discusses Psalm 45, in which he sees the birth of Christ. He shows that this messianic psalm describes Christ as a mighty warrior and king. The psalm goes on to describe him as a beautiful bridegroom who brings forth many children. Lewis then pauses to note the peculiarity of associating these images with a newborn child. An infant does not appear to be a king, a giant killer, a bridegroom, or a father. Even less does an infant child appear to be the eternal Word (*Logos*).[4] The incarnate Christ exceeds all of our expectations.

Lewis's examples demonstrate a deep understanding both of Scripture and of Christ. This child is far greater than outward appearances indicate. Without divine revelation, His identity would have remained unknown, but through Scripture, we see the richness and complexity of the Christ. Lewis expands on this. Christ is a warrior, but in his parenthetical explanation, Lewis recasts Him as "giant killer," introducing an image evocative both of a biblical theme (David slaying Goliath) and a fairy tale (Jack and the beanstalk) to explain Christ's power.

Jewish Heritage

In the incarnation, God took a real human nature. He was born into a specific culture. Lewis stresses this Jewish heritage when he notes Jesus' use of Hebrew poetry. Christ's knowledge and use of this genre is not miraculous, but it comes through the most normal of means. As part of His incarnation, He took on a human heredity and underwent ordinary, human development. Christ learned from the culture surrounding Him, but in all likelihood, such knowledge came most directly from His mother.[5]

This simple explanation underscores the humanity of Christ. Normal heredity and developmental factors exercised their natural influence upon Him. He learned from His surroundings and particularly from Mary. This cultural background is reflected in Christ's teaching. Because the ethics and beliefs of His culture were based on divine revelation, He did not produce many innovations.[6] He continued to follow in the same pattern as most Jewish teachers. Any attempt to understand the Christ apart from His Jewish heritage will miss crucial features.

Christ the Archetypal Man

While Jesus was incarnate as a specific person within this specific Jewish culture, Lewis also saw Him as the universal, archetypal Man. This is particularly evident in the title that Jesus often used of Himself: the Son of Man. Lewis understands this messianic title to mean *the* Man or the Archetypal Man who is connected to all humanity. Because of His unique status, His suffering and His triumphs may be shared by all people. Lewis believes that the humanity of Christ is often neglected by those who focus almost exclusively on His deity. Some may stress His godhead so strongly that they fail to proclaim that the Savior remains incarnate. He will never abandon His triumphant, glorified human nature. The person and work of Christ are also misrepresented by those who overly stress one nature in certain events. For example, depictions of Christmas may stress the humanity to the exclusion of His deity. On the other hand, many ignore His human nature after the resurrection. The entire work of Christ is performed by the God-man. These acts are not only powerful acts of God. He has also given us the benefits of this work, and in Him, all humanity is triumphant.[7] Lewis clearly proclaims the enduring humanity of the Christ, which ennobles all humanity. Christ is both God and Man, and His work is accomplished by both natures.

Perfection

Although He is fully human, Christ is also unique. He claimed to be perfect and sinless, something unattainable for the rest of humanity. These claims help us see His full identity. In a passage similar to his arguments in *Mere Christianity*, Lewis writes that Christ denied that He was sinful or had ever committed sins. Additionally, when He says that He is meek and humble, people believe Him. Lewis sees this as an argument for Christ's deity. If His claim of sinfulness is not true, it is extremely arrogant, yet He is seldom considered to be an arrogant man. Humanity's reactions to Jesus' claims may, to some degree, show the truthfulness of the statements. The only explanation that fully accounts for Jesus' claims, and for human acceptance of His goodness, is to believe that His claims are true.[8]

Christ is a human being, yet He is fundamentally different. Because nothing is truly analogous to the incarnation, Christ exhibits differences from the rest of humanity, such as perfection and sinlessness.

THE WORK OF CHRIST

CHRIST THE REDEEMER

The incarnate Christ comes to redeem His people. This is seen in a "second meaning" of Psalm 49. Lewis focuses on verses 7 and 8, which read: "No man can redeem the life of another or give to God a ransom for him—the ransom for a life is costly, no payment is ever enough." Lewis comments on these verses, noting their connection to Christ's work. Only the Son of God was good enough to pay the price of salvation. He particularly focuses on the word "redeem," saying that this strengthens the effect of the image. Although this word is now used almost exclusively in a theological context, it is essentially a financial term. The price of this redemption was too high for anyone else to pay, but the Savior did pay it for all people when He died on the cross.[9] It is remarkable to see Lewis using this type of language. He frequently shuns similar descriptions of the atonement. Here he declares that Christ pays the price, once for all, on Calvary, and only Christ is fit to do this.

CHRIST THE SUFFERING KING

Further descriptions of Christ's work are seen as Lewis continues to look for second, or deeper, meanings in the Psalms. Here he focuses on two figures revealed in the Psalter: the sufferer and the victorious king. Lewis maintains that the sufferer was frequently seen as a personification of the entire nation of Israel. In contrast, the victor-king was the son and successor of David: the promised Messiah. Christ did not choose one of these images, but He is identified with both of them.[10]

The combination of these two disparate figures is striking. Lewis notes the personification of Israel and Christ's self-identification with that personification. The Psalms provide essential information about the Messiah. Not only is He the Son of David, but He also comes to suffer.

Lewis continues to explore Christ's kingly status in Psalm 110. Lewis frequently cites this passage, here using it to explain the correspondence between Christ and Melchizedek. Melchizedek was both a priest and a king. While this was a common combination in some cultures, it was unknown in ancient Israel. Because kings were descended from David, they belonged to the tribe of Judah. In contrast, priests were descendants of Levi. The offices were mutually exclusive. Melchizedek is exempt from this regulation because he lived before Judah and Levi. So also Christ existed before these patriarchs, and so, like Melchizedek, He can be both a priest and a king.[11] While Lewis does not fully discuss the parallels between Melchizedek and Christ, he highlights their primary similarity. Melchizedek and Christ are both royal priests.

CHRIST THE TEACHER

Another aspect of Christ's work is His office as teacher. Certainly, Christ is not merely a teacher, yet education was a significant feature of His ministry. As Lewis examines Jesus' teaching, he notes that while it is perfect, it is also complex. The teachings of Jesus are not organized into a perfect system. He did not write a book Himself; the Gospels were written by others. Many of Christ's recorded sayings were given as answers to specific questions and are connected to their context. Indeed, His words are not academic lectures; instead, they are preaching. Consequently, Christ's teaching cannot be mastered by the intellect alone. He is not merely trying to convey a body of knowledge, He is transforming us. His teachings are not grasped by the mind alone but by the heart.[12]

Christ is much more complex than many would make Him. One cannot fully master His teachings, and He cannot be contained. Lewis tried to maintain that complexity and richness, not minimize it.

CHRIST THE EXAMPLE

Lewis considers the person and work of Christ in great detail, but the discussion is not complete unless it is applied. An important element of Christ's work is that of providing an example. Of course, Jesus is not merely an example, but He does provide a model for His people. Lewis shows the significance of this example as he considers how we should act when we come into contact with bad people. Our Lord came to people in difficult circumstances and treated them with humility and love. He was unconcerned with the effect this might have on His reputation or about how others might interpret His actions. Christ spoke with the scandalous Samaritan woman who met Him at the well. He protected the woman caught in adultery and forgave her sin. He entered the homes of tax collectors and sinners and even shared table fellowship with them. This is the example that Jesus provides for us.[13]

CHRIST TYPES IN OTHER CULTURES

One final aspect of Lewis's Christology is evident in his work on the Psalms. As he discusses second meanings in the Psalms, he also considers several extrabiblical accounts of Christ figures. The first regards a section of the *Republic* in which Plato describes a perfectly righteous man who is treated in an incomprehensibly barbaric manner. He is unjustly bound, scourged, and finally impaled (a death Lewis equates with crucifixion). In all likelihood, the inspiration for this passage was the death of Socrates. Plato believed that the death of his master was unjust, thus he graphically demonstrated how a corrupt world often treats goodness that it cannot understand. For Plato, the violent death of the righteous man illustrated and emphasized the wickedness of killing Socrates.

A Christian who reads this passage, however, may see it in a different light. It may be grounded in the death of Socrates, but it appears to have more in common with the death of Christ. How can one not see a parallel to the binding, scourging, and crucifixion of Jesus? Where else would one find a truly righteous man in this sinful earth? Yet Plato, a pagan who wrote some 350 years before Christ, could not really be writing of the Messiah, could he? Lewis tries to reconcile these things, saying that Plato is writing about the way this wicked world treats goodness. This happens on many levels, but the greatest example of this injustice is the crucifixion. Both Socrates and Christ faced death (though Socrates died more peacefully) for the same reason. Good people are willing to stand up for the truth, and our fallen world is eager to crush them. Plato, after witnessing the unjust death of his master, discussed the highest expression of this reality. Because he did this, his writing parallels the true fulfillment of how perfect goodness is treated in this world: Christ. Plato was able to do this because it is a reflection of truth. However, Lewis does not see this as an instance of God's direct revelation. Plato likely believed that he was providing an example of this world's evil. He did not imagine that he was anticipating the perfect example of an unjust execution.[14]

Plato's impaled righteous man and Christ are related because of the goodness of the victim. It is the nature of this world to destroy goodness, whether the imperfect goodness of Plato's victim, or Socrates, or the perfection of Christ. Far from detracting from Christ, Plato's righteous man prefigures Christ, thus the truth of his writing endures. The most poignant illustration of the world's tendency to destroy goodness is found in Christ crucified.

Lewis also alludes to other striking parallels between paganism and Christianity. Again he refers to "Corn-kings," or harvest deities who die and return to life again to bring life to the world, nature, or people.[15] Lewis notes three primary interpretations of these parallels. The first is an anthropological approach, which considers the parallels to be indicative of a common origin. All myth draws from common experience and expresses similar understandings. According to this view, Christianity offers nothing unique. The second approach is that of some early Christian fathers who considered such myths to be of satanic origin. The third approach mediates these two extremes. It maintains that mythology may contain divine or demonic elements. It also fulfills a human longing for stories. These myths may display elements of the truth because God permits them to do so. The truth may not be portrayed as precisely or as accurately as in other sources, yet they still may reflect that truth.[16]

Lewis believes that pagan parallels are an expression of divine truth, yet this does not diminish Christianity. Parallels are evident, but the Gospel is the highest expression of truth. The greatest understanding belongs to those who see the fulfillment of the myths. Looking at these myths through Christ, we see a connection that the ancient authors of these stories could not see. We may see the highest example of these patterns in Christ. Lewis maintained that this is not simply an example of projecting our wishes on older stories nor of wishful thinking. There is a real connection between these events. This is so strong that Lewis imagines that if the producers of these myths saw the fulfillment in Christ, they might well identify Him as the true subject of their words.[17]

Reflections on the Psalms provides a broad picture of the person and work of Christ, prefigured in mythology and in the inspired and inerrant prophecies of the Old Testament. Both serve similar purposes but employ different methodology.

THE FOUR LOVES

Lewis's second devotional work, *The Four Loves*, draws on many different aspects of his life. Using his linguistic skills, Lewis distinguishes four different Greek words for love, translating them as affection, friendship, romantic love, and charity. This book was written late in his life, after his marriage. Lewis's personal experiences are joined with his spiritual reflection to produce a significant work on love.

Lewis explains the proper understanding and role of each of these loves and places them in a Christian context. *The Four Loves* discusses many different aspects of love, including the love we see in Christ Jesus. While this is not a book about Christology, a Christian cannot discuss true love without reference to the work of Christ. The greatest example of God's love for us is seen in Christ.

DEITY OF CHRIST

While Christ's deity is defended by apologetics in other books by Lewis, here it is simply proclaimed as an assumed fact. On the first page of this book, Lewis writes that God's love is the perfect example of gift-love (*agape*). The highest example of this is seen in the trinitarian relationship. The Father and the Son give themselves completely to each other. The Son gives Himself to the world and gives His life for the world.[18] This love is uncompromising and absolute, each person giving everything to the other. In this love there is no distinction of rank or honor. Within the unity of the Trinity, the Father and the Son are both fully divine.

HUMANITY OF CHRIST

The divine Christ is also a real human being. Lewis upholds the uniqueness and perfection of Christ, as evidenced by his discussion of affection. Lewis notes that, in their sinfulness, all human beings have tainted this love with selfishness. This is so pervasive that we consider our sinful attitudes and actions to be normal. By nature, we express greed, egocentrism, self-deception, and self-pity. We would hardly describe someone who lacks these defects as "normal." But in this way, Christ is different from other humans. He does not exhibit these sinful characteristics, so, in the judgment of the world, He is abnormal. This explains the willingness and eagerness of the world to reject and kill Him. When humanity encountered perfection in Christ, we responded by saying that He was demon-possessed. Ultimately, we crucified Him.[19] The incarnate Christ was unique in His sinlessness; consequently, the world rejected Him. In most other ways, He was like any other human being.

Being fully human, Jesus expressed natural human loves. One way was in His patriotism. Lewis sees Christ's lament over Jerusalem as proof of this. Jesus did not want to see harm come to His country, thus He spoke words of concern for His people. Jesus also expressed deep love for His friends. To highlight this, Lewis reflects on St. Augustine's despair at the death of a friend. Augustine noted that giving one's heart to anything except God leads to despair. Unless the human soul is turned to God, it is inevitably joined to sorrow.[20] Lewis responds that this is more reflective of the philosophies that Augustine followed before his conversion than it is of Christianity itself. The Christian faith does not call us away from human relationships. Instead, we see Jesus, who is deeply involved in human relationships. The rejection and stubbornness of Jerusalem moved Him to tears, as did the death of His friend Lazarus. He loved all people, yet one disciple in particular is identified as the one He loved.[21]

Jesus loved, grieved, and wept. Perhaps the strongest emotions faced by Christ were those accompanying the crucifixion. While we seek to avoid such suffering and heartbreak, God does not promise that we will be free of these pains. Even Christ faced them, calling out on the cross, "Why have You forsaken Me?" Such emotions demonstrate Christ's true humanity.

THE ULTIMATE LOVE OF CHRIST

Lewis reveals more of his thinking as he describes the love of Christ for His creation. God's love is far beyond our love because He is the source of all other loves. In His perfection, there is nothing that He needs. He does not need us, our gifts, or our love. He does not come to us seeking things for Himself, but only seeks to give us His gifts.[22] The full extent of His gracious love is revealed in God's actions toward humanity. In His omniscience, God knew what humanity would do, even before we existed. He loved us so deeply that He made us, already seeing

> the buzzing cloud of flies about the cross, the flayed back pressed against the uneven stake, the nails driven through the mesial nerves, the repeated incipient suffocation as the body droops, the repeated torture of back and arms as it is time after time, for breath's sake, hitched up.[23]

Lewis goes so far as to compare God to a being that deliberately chooses and makes parasites who will use and exploit Him. God fully knows what we will do, yet He still causes our existence. This is the ultimate example of love because it is the work of God who Himself is love. This concept is the heart of *The Four Loves*. So complete is God's love that He creates, despite knowing what His creation would do to Him. The sacrifice of Christ was not an accidental event. It was planned and forechosen by a willing victim.

IMITATION OF HIS LOVE

Christ's love, which transforms us, provides an example for us to emulate. While we cannot live up to Christ's example, we can follow Him. We are called to imitate the incarnate God not only in His passion and vicarious suffering for others, but in all aspects of His perfect life. His vocation as a carpenter, His actions as He walked the roads of Israel, His response to the crowds, His reaction to opposition, even the way He dealt with interruptions and a lack of privacy, all of these things are examples to us.[24] The Son of God became a human being to serve human beings. His people are called to follow His example. Lewis envisions a broad imitation not merely in large and dramatic gestures, but at all times and in small actions.

One particular human love that allows us to follow Christ's example is found in the marriage relationship. Here Lewis considers the challenging words of Ephesians 5. As he looks at these verses, he emphasizes the character of marriage and its parallels to the relationship of Christ and the church. Lewis reminds us that the husband is called to love his wife as Christ loved the church, even to the point of death. Thus, the love of a husband for his wife is not a relationship of convenience or of simple emotion.

This love is giving and self-sacrificing, revealing its depth more in the challenges, sorrows, and suffering of marriage than in its joys. Like St. Paul, Lewis sees the ultimate fulfillment of this love only in Christ. The Savior does not choose the church because of her beauty or value. In fact, He chooses her despite her failures and flaws, seeing the perfect bride that He might make her to be through His love. This is the model of love that Ephesians, and Lewis, upholds. The Christian husband is, likewise, called to gracious, self-sacrificing love.[25]

Lewis does not retreat from these verses or downplay the theme of headship. Neither does he allow the headship of the husband without a Christlike character. This headship is selfless. It may involve suffering and forgiveness, and it certainly is carried out in love. Only when a husband emulates the example of Christ is Lewis willing to concede headship. There can be no headship apart from the imitation of Christ's absolute giving love.

Transformation of Love

When he began, Lewis intended to write a book that showed the superiority of gift-love to need-love. He quickly modified this, realizing that many need-based loves may also be valuable and noble. Still the perfect gift-love, demonstrated by God in Christ Jesus, is the supreme example of love. Lewis concludes *The Four Loves* by discussing how various loves may be transformed and ennobled. Affection, friendship, and even romantic love all remain, but they can become modes of expressing the deepest love: charity. Lewis compares this transformation to the incarnation. The perfectly divine Son has taken a perfect human nature into Himself. This did not diminish His deity, but it ennobled humanity. In the same way, lesser human loves may be taken up into charity and used for divine ends. They still remain natural loves, but they may also be expressions of God's perfect love as well.[26] As the incarnation raised and ennobled humanity, so natural love is perfected when it becomes an imitation of God's love and of God, who is love Himself. *The Four Loves* provides Lewis's meditative comments on love and, tangentially, on the person and work of Christ. We know love when we know Christ, and if we know Him, we will seek to emulate His love.

LETTERS TO MALCOLM

Throughout his life, C. S. Lewis maintained a lively correspondence with many people. Early in his career, he penned a fictional correspondence in his highly successful book *The Screwtape Letters*. In *Letters to Malcolm: Chiefly on Prayer*, the last book he wrote, Lewis again produced a fictional correspondence to present his theological ideas. Through his letters, Lewis discusses a variety of subjects, but primarily, as the title indicates, he focuses on the topic of prayer. As in his other theological works, Lewis includes his understandings of Christ Jesus.

THE TRAGIC REDEEMER

Throughout this book, Lewis stresses the omnipotence of God, particularly as it is evident in His creation. We pray to Almighty God who not only deserves prayer, but is powerful enough to answer. His power is evident in His work, particularly in His creation. Yet even in this expression of God's power, we see that He uses His power in a most surprising way. He knows what will become of His creation. Even before He has created this universe, He knows that its salvation will require the incarnation, suffering, and death of His Son. Lewis, thus, questions whether we might see an element of tragedy in God's act of creation.[27]

Here, as in *The Four Loves*, Lewis reflects on God's foreknowledge. He is the Tragic Creator because He foreknew the fall and the cost of our redemption. God's love is demonstrated in His willingness to create, despite knowing the pain it would cause.

THE INCARNATION

God responded to our human condition by becoming one of us. Here, as in the rest of his writings, Lewis holds to the creedal proposition that the incarnation did not lower God but raised humanity. Thus, in the incarnation, the Son of God takes on an entire human nature, both body and soul. Christ also assumed everything that it means to be human; our limitations, sorrows, frustrations, labors, struggles, and even our mortality are taken up into the Godhead.[28] Because of the incarnation, God Himself has directly experienced these things. All these limitations and deficiencies, all the effects of our sin and rebellion, have been taken up and are intimately known by Him. The darkness of our world has been taken into the pure light of God, where it is swallowed up and defeated. Darkness cannot overcome Christ's light.

The incarnation, which allows God to experience human weakness, also ennobles humanity. God has taken our nature into Himself. Consequently, Lewis notes, we now may say that all people partially resemble Christ. Lewis does not tie this to the doctrines of creation and the image of God, but to the incarnation. While this point is not often presented, Lewis remarks that we find it easy to make the association. In evidence of this, Lewis refers to a European pastor who had seen Hitler. Humanly speaking, this man had ample reason to hate Hitler, but when asked about Hitler's appearance, the pastor remarked that Hitler looked like all other men, and, therefore, he looked like Christ.[29] This startling statement is a remarkable confession of the true humanity of Christ. He has taken humanity up into Himself, though, of course, with significant differences.

IMAGES OF CHRIST

The incarnation has implications for prayer. As people pray, Lewis notes, they will likely envision an image of God. However, this immediately presents a difficulty. There are no adequate images for either the Father or the Holy Spirit. Any mental image of these two persons falls short of reality. The situation is different with Christ, however. He became human—a form that can be imagined. This may lead to a Christocentricity in prayer that Lewis finds inappropriate. It may be that envisioning the incarnate God may lead to prayers that are exclusively addressed to the Son, with a de-emphasis of the Father and the Holy Spirit.[30] This depiction is natural and may be helpful, yet Lewis cautions that we not forget the rest of the Trinity.

At one point, Lewis notes a personal difficulty with images. St. Ignatius encouraged people to visualize Bible scenes as part of their meditation. Lewis found this ineffective. He knew that his mental picture was inaccurate, so he imagined additional details of the scene and, through this, was distracted from his prayers. But the crucifixion did not lead him into these mental elaborations of trivial details. When imagined in its gory reality, the staggering horror of the crucifixion crushes all other thoughts. Even such salutary emotions as compassion or gratitude are eclipsed by the horror of this death. This death is a reality that must be faced, but no human can live with these frightful images indefinitely. As evidence of this, Lewis notes that the crucifixion was seldom depicted in Christian art while crucifixions were still being performed. Only after the terrifying reality of death by crucifixion had passed away could artists depict the scene of Christ's death in devotional pictures or crucifixes.[31]

The crucifixion, while necessary, is horrible and cannot be lived with, yet it must be faced. This is particularly true because all of God's actions toward humanity, including the crucifixion, are undertaken for us personally. Lewis reflects on the frequent speculation that Christ, who came to suffer and die for the entire world, would have carried out this same salvation even if it were only for one person. Lewis expands this line of thought, wondering if even the creation itself might be seen as the gracious work of God—a work that He would have done even for one individual.[32] Seen this way, each person, perhaps even each particle of matter, is valued by God. Whether this is the case or not, the passion of Christ demonstrates how highly God values us. Christ's suffering was undertaken for us.

Lewis has further cause to reflect on what Christ has done for us when he considers Jesus' prayer and agony in the Garden of Gethsemane. Jesus' frequent predictions of His passion make it clear that He had foreseen His own death. He knew that His words and actions would lead Him to His execution. Yet somehow, Lewis maintains, this knowledge must have been absent when He offered His prayer in the garden. Christ would not have been able to pray to avoid the suffering while simultaneously knowing that it was necessary. He would have not asked for something contrary to His Father's will. In this withdrawn knowledge, Lewis sees that Christ is living with the entire human situation. He experiences every trial, frustration, and difficulty faced by human beings. He faces a horrible death and is granted a time of possible escape. He has one final hope that He might be spared this death. Indeed, Lewis suggests that the story of Abraham's near-sacrifice of Isaac might have been seen as a precedent. Perhaps obedience was the only thing necessary, and death itself could be avoided. This struggle regarding a possible escape is one more indication of Christ's true humanity.[33]

In considering these events, Lewis first addresses the two natures of Christ. If Christ, as God, is omniscient, how can He pray for something that He knows will not happen? If He has fore-knowledge, why does He pray? Lewis does not resolve this, other than to say that the knowledge must somehow have been with-drawn. Christ faced all trials and sufferings. He hoped and prayed for escape from the suffering. This agonizing prayer and hope against hope are evidence of His true humanity.

This very point makes Gethsemane relevant to Lewis. The suffering of Christ in the garden is indicative of what it means to be human. We know that we may have to suffer and try to accept afflictions in humble submission when this is necessary. Yet we also should know that struggling with afflictions may be part of God's will and an appropriate human reaction. Christ, the perfect man, struggled with the cup that was placed before Him. He sought a way out of the suffering, if it were possible. If the perfect man faces anxiety in the face of suffering, so can we. We are not Stoics, embracing suffering as a normal part of life. We can strug-gle with the difficulties of suffering.[34] *Letters to Malcolm* was writ-ten after Joy Lewis's death and near the end of Lewis's life. He had experienced great grief and hardship. He had prayed unfulfilled prayers. Thus, the reflection on Christ was especially meaningful. If He experienced these emotions, others may experience them also.

Throughout his Christian life, but particularly in his later years, Lewis was interested in connecting the work, and particu-larly the passion, of Christ to human suffering. Christ's suffering demonstrates His humanity. Because He is like us in every way, He suffers. In fact, Lewis thinks that every element of Christ's passion shows common human suffering raised to its highest intensity. Jesus prays for deliverance from these pains, but His request is denied. He seeks the strength and support of His friends in this time of crisis only to find that they have fallen asleep, just as our friends may fail us in time of need. Christ goes before the church that He created and it condemns Him to death. When every human avenue of help has been exhausted, Jesus turns to God Himself. Yet the last living words that the incarnate God speaks are, "Why have You forsaken Me?" Humans frequently face these smaller trials, but the Messiah faced them in their full ferocity. Every person, each institution, all possible hopes failed Him.[35]

Christ, being the archetypal Man, experienced all of this. He has undergone all that we have to face and more, even being forsaken by God. Christ faced every human frustration and suffering, intensified to their highest level. While this may appear bleak, it was a great comfort to Lewis in his own suffering. Christ has gone before us in suffering.

Lewis knew that life is often difficult, but he did not avoid or ignore the challenges. Having faced suffering, he could comfort others. So Lewis assures his readers that they do not need to feel guilty if the prospect of suffering causes them anxiety. It is natural to want to avoid suffering. The anxiety that we feel in the face of pain is not sin, but it is an affliction. When we face such trials in faith, they are connected to the passion of Christ.[36] Afflictions are not willingly chosen, yet when they arise, they can be transformed in the life of the Christian. The suffering of Christians is directly related to the suffering of Christ. It is a sharing of His passion.

CONCLUSION

Lewis's devotional works provide a look into his Christian life and understanding. The Christology they present is anchored in the creeds and applied to both the author and the reader. The greatest applications of Christology are in the ennobling of humanity through the incarnation and in the connection between the suffering of Christ and of Christians. As he claimed he would do, Lewis "fed on the truth" and invited his readers to the table.

NOTES

1. C. S. Lewis, *Reflections on the Psalms* (New York: Harcourt, Brace, Jovanovich, 1958), 7.
2. Ibid., 1.
3. Ibid., 116.
4. Ibid., 130.
5. Ibid., 5–6.
6. Ibid., 26, 27.
7. Ibid., 133–34.
8. Ibid., 135–136.
9. Ibid., 35.
10. Ibid., 120–21.

11. Ibid., 123.
12. Ibid., 111–12, 119.
13. Ibid., 68–69.
14. Ibid., 104, 105.
15. Ibid., 105.
16. Ibid., 106, 107.
17. Ibid., 108.
18. C. S. Lewis, *The Four Loves* (New York: Harcourt, Brace, Jovanovich, 1960), 11.
19. Ibid., 81.
20. Augustine, *Confessions*, IV–X.
21. Lewis, *Four Loves*, 167.
22. Ibid., 175.
23. Ibid., 177.
24. Ibid., 17.
25. Ibid., 148, 149.
26. Ibid., 184.
27. C. S. Lewis, *Letters to Malcolm: Chiefly on Prayer* (New York: Harcourt, Brace, Jovanovich, 1963), 91.
28. Ibid., 70–71.
29. Ibid., 84.
30. Ibid.
31. Ibid., 85.
32. Ibid., 55.
33. Ibid., 42.
34. Ibid., 42–43.
35. Ibid., 43.
36. Ibid., 41.

Chapter Twelve

Personal Works

C. S. Lewis was a prolific and varied writer. In his apologetic works, he proclaims and defends the Christian faith. In his fictional writings, he presents and recasts that faith in new forms. His devotional works allow him to ponder the meaning and application of Christianity. All these share a common theology. He writes of a God who is greater than we, who will not be tamed by our limitations but who mercifully comes to us. This God is also seen in the final category of Lewis's works: his personal writings. Two of these, *The Pilgrim's Regress* and *Surprised by Joy*, are autobiographical accounts of his early life and conversion. *A Grief Observed* chronicles his mourning at the death of his wife. Finally, Lewis's correspondence covers a large period of his life. In all these writings, we glimpse the private life of C. S. Lewis and see reflections of his theological understanding.

AUTOBIOGRAPHICAL WORKS

THE PILGRIM'S REGRESS

When C. S. Lewis became a Christian, he quickly realized that he needed to tell the story of his conversion. In an effort to make the story more engaging, he wrote an allegory patterned after Bunyan's *The Pilgrim's Progress*. In this transparent narrative, the protagonist, John, is born in Puritania, where he is taught to fear the Landlord. This is difficult because the Landlord has imposed many impossible rules. John leaves his native Puritania to meet Mr. Enlightenment, who denies that there is a Landlord. John becomes imprisoned by the Spirit of the Age, only to be rescued by Reason. Eventually, John meets Mother Kirk, who directs him to the Landlord's Island. Although there are subtle points to the allegory, the main correlations are obvious.

The story relates Lewis's path to Christianity, focusing primarily on his pre-Christian life. Because of this, there is little mention of Christ, "the Landlord's Son." Indeed, there are only four specific allusions. The first paraphrases Jesus' words as He washed His disciples' feet (John 13), attributing these words to the Landlord's Son.[1] Again, Christ is mentioned as Death tries to frighten John. Death says that the Landlord's Son, who is otherwise fearless, was afraid to die,[2] reflecting Christ's anguish in Gethsemane. The third reference to Christ regards His humanity. John asks Virtue if it is wrong to be ashamed of one's physical, human body. The response given is that the Landlord's Son did not feel shame at His humanity. When John says that the incarnation was a special case, Virtue answers that this is because Christ is the archetypal man.[3] In the incarnation, Christ became the archetypal man. He was not ashamed of His humanity, nor is it the cause of sinfulness.

The fourth reference is the most significant. A large portion of *The Pilgrim's Regress* presents Lewis's conception of the fulfillment of pagan mythology within Christianity. Lewis writes of the Rules, which the Shepherd People (the Jews) were given, and of the pictures (myths), which the pagans knew. In isolation, both the rules and the pictures are dangerous. Ideally, a person would not be left to do this but would, instead, find "Mother Kirk" at the beginning. Living with Mother Kirk, one might learn something entirely new that has been brought by the Landlord's Son. This new thing is neither the rules nor the pictures, and when you have it, the rules and the pictures are both seen in proper perspective.[4]

The Landlord's Son is the revealer of that which is neither the rules nor the pictures. Christ's revelation was not a repristination of the Law or of pagan mythology but something different— the Gospel. This further revelation does not refute either the Law or mythology, but it brings them to fuller life and greater understanding.

One must question the infrequency of references to Christ within an autobiographical account of a man's conversion. Explanation may be found in the nature of Lewis's conversion. When Lewis spoke of his conversion, he often was referring to his conversion to theism, which occurred in 1929. He did not become a Christian until 1931. *The Pilgrim's Regress* was published in 1933. Christ is present in the book; His incarnation, life, and ministry are noted, but He is seen as little more than a revealer. Lewis is mainly concerned with presenting the events that prepared him for Christ's message.

SURPRISED BY JOY

Lewis corrected this weakness 22 years later in his second autobiography. By this time, Lewis was well known as a Christian writer and speaker. Repeatedly asked about his conversion from atheism, Lewis realized that *The Pilgrim's Regress* was inadequate. In fact, in the preface to the third edition of that book, he noted that it was needlessly obscure and had an uncharitable temper.[5] In response, Lewis prepared *Surprised by Joy: The Shape of My Early Life*. Like *The Pilgrim's Regress*, this book recounts Lewis's life until his conversion. There is a heavy emphasis on Lewis's childhood, adolescence, and education because these help contextualize his rejection of Christianity (which occurred at age 13) and his later conversion. Like *The Pilgrim's Regress*, *Surprised by Joy* has less Christological material than might be expected, yet references to Christ are much more explicit than in Lewis's earlier work.

Shortly before his 10th birthday, Lewis's mother died despite his prayers for her recovery. In and of itself, this did not lead him to reject God. Indeed, his reaction shows a general apathy toward the divine. Prayer had been a mechanical exercise. He did not fear God nor hold Him in awe; He was neither Savior nor Judge. Instead, the young Lewis had asked for God's power as if He was a magician to be manipulated. Lewis had no thought of an ongoing faith relationship or concern for who God really was. He wanted God to perform a miracle at his request, then disappear.[6]

God existed for Lewis, but He had little relevance. It is interesting that the roles Lewis failed to ascribe to God—Savior and Judge—are both part of the work of Christ. Much of *Surprised by Joy* recounts Lewis's departure from the Christian faith and, therefore, ignores Christ. As he moves closer to faith, references to Christ increase. One event was of pivotal importance. Lewis describes a conversation that he had with an avowed atheist. This nonbeliever casually remarked that there was good evidence to support the historicity of the Christian Gospels. He compared this to the many stories of Corn kings and gods who die to rise again, stories that could be found in Sir James Frazer's *The Golden Bough*. This atheist concluded that it almost appeared as if, in Jesus, this story had actually occurred. This startling admission shook Lewis. He was unsettled by this evaluation of the historical evidence for the Gospels. If this skeptic was impressed by the evidence for Christianity, there must be something to it.[7] The combination of historical truth with the mythology of the Dying God was compelling.

Three years later, Lewis reluctantly confessed his faith in God. However, he explains, he was not yet a Christian. He had become a simple theist, believing in God but not yet believing in the incarnation.[8] In recounting this first conversion, Lewis evaluates it in Christological terms. What distinguishes Christianity from theism is the incarnate Christ.

The bulk of *Surprised by Joy* is concerned with Lewis's life until his conversion to theism. The final chapter briefly describes his progress to Christianity. Lewis looked for a religion in which the hints of paganism were fulfilled and found two possibilities: Christianity and Hinduism. He rejected Hinduism for two reasons. The first reason was that Hinduism seemed to combine philosophy and paganism, but it did not evaluate either element or reconcile contradictory elements. Lewis compares this to a mixing of oil and water. They both exist, but they are not united. The second reason for his rejection of Hinduism was that it lacked the historicity of Christianity.[9]

This deduction led Lewis once more to the primary sources for Christianity—the Gospels. Lewis writes that he now knew that the Gospels were not mythological. They lacked the character of myth that he saw in other writings. Surprisingly, however, the content of Christianity was similar to the content of many of the great myths. The critical difference is that Christianity presented this material in a historical context. Lewis summarized the differences between Christianity and mythology, saying,

If ever a myth had become fact, had been incarnated, it would be just like this. And nothing else in all literature was just like this. ... [N]o person was like the Person it depicted. ... Here and here only in all time the myth must have become fact; the Word, flesh; God, Man. This is not "a religion," nor "a philosophy." It is the summing up and actuality of them all.[10]

Lewis's examination of the evidence led him to Christianity. Here, he saw the fulfillment of pagan mythology. What he saw made sense, and it was unique. Lewis became a Christian when he saw the reality of the incarnation. He believed that Jesus was the Son of God.

Surprised by Joy and *The Pilgrim's Regress* both tell the story of Lewis's conversion, though in different forms. When the two are compared, we see a development of Lewis's Christian thought and a deeper understanding and acknowledgment of Christ.

A GRIEF OBSERVED

While *A Grief Observed* is not, properly speaking, autobiographical, it is of such a personal nature, and is so revealing of Lewis's private thoughts, that it should be considered with his autobiographical works. The relationship between Jack and Joy Lewis has been the subject of intense interest and scrutiny. They were married in a civil ceremony in 1956 to allow Joy (an American citizen) to remain in England, but they did not live as husband and wife. In early 1957, Joy was diagnosed with terminal bone cancer. The following March, with Joy hospitalized and on her deathbed, they were married in a Christian ceremony. Remarkably, Joy recovered, only to see the cancer return two years later. When Joy died on July 13, 1960, Lewis was devastated. Working through his grief, he kept a journal, which was published in 1961.

A Grief Observed chronicles the pain, frustration, and anger of a grieving man. Lewis wrestles with his ideas about God, justice, and suffering. In *The Problem of Pain*, he had looked at the challenge of suffering in generic and philosophical terms. In *A Grief Observed*, it becomes specific and personal. While this book reveals much about grief and about Lewis, we look for one key element—how does Christ appear in Lewis's grief?

That question must be considered in the context of the personal crisis Lewis faced. Since his conversion had involved a detailed consideration of the evidence for Christainity, he was not in danger of denying God's existence. Rather, the impending crisis had to do with the nature of God. Could it be that the God who truly existed was neither loving nor merciful, but sadistic and cruel? The possibility of this conclusion was frightening.[11] This crisis caused Lewis to reassess his faith. Lewis often wrote of Christ as the archetypal man. This has ramifications for human suffering. If He faced trials, it is only natural that other people will also. A Christian's suffering may even be understood as a participation in the suffering of Christ. Lewis notes the connection but feels no consolation from it. At the time he most needs help, God appears silent. When he expressed these ideas to a clergyman, he was reminded that Christ also had the same experience. When the Son of God was crucified, He cried out to His Father, "Why have You forsaken Me?" Hearing those familiar words, however, brought Lewis no comfort. The words were true, but they didn't ease his suffering.[12]

The solution that Lewis used to console others fell short of his expectations. He remained aware of this aid, but he took no comfort from it. Later, in frustration, he asks why we should believe that God is good. The frustrations and suffering of life seem to argue against His goodness. How can our pain be reconciled with His goodness? As an answer, most Christians would speak of Christ who comes to suffer for us and show God's mercy. Yet Lewis is not comforted by this. What if even Jesus had been deceived by God? After all, in His pain, He asked why God had forsaken Him. Could it be that God really was cruel? That He had sadistically planned to deceive the Christ and others?[13]

Lewis identifies with Christ's forsakenness. Yet even this gives him no consolation. If Christ was forsaken, what might the rest of humanity expect? Lewis would later call such speculation "filth and nonsense,"[14] but here he struggles. Logical reasoning provides far less consolation than he had expected. There is no escape from grief. It cannot be avoided or ignored. The Christian faith may provide comfort to the grieving, but it neither nullifies the sense of temporal loss nor necessarily removes the pain of mourning.

The other references to Christ in *A Grief Observed* concern images. Near the end of the book, Lewis complains that all the photographs of his wife are bad, but he explains that all images, whether photographed or imagined, fall short of reality. Drawing a parallel, he talks about the Lord's Supper. In the Sacrament, he is given a small, tasteless wafer and is told that it is the body of Christ. He questions whether the lack of resemblance between these two things is an advantage. If the wafer appeared more like the actual body of Christ, Lewis thought it might be harder to believe the eucharistic presence. It is not an image that he craves, but the reality of Christ. In the same way, it was his wife that he needed, not her picture.[15]

This is the first expression of a need for Christ in this book. Lewis struggles with his faith and returns not to reasoned arguments, but to Christ Himself. It is not the outward appearance of the Sacrament, but Christ Himself that Lewis craves. He continues to discuss images, saying that the popularity of images shows that they have a purpose, but he is concerned by a potential problem. It is a small step from having an image of something holy to having a Holy Image. Nowhere is this more true than in our conception of God Himself. It is all too easy to assume that one's personal ideas about God are identical with God Himself. He comes and breaks those images because He exceeds them. They are too limited to accurately reflect the Godhead. Lewis speculates that one of the signs that God is truly present is His shattering of our limited human conceptions. "The Incarnation is the supreme example; it leaves all previous ideas of the Messiah in ruins."[16] The reality of God exceeds all expectations. The incarnation shattered human ideas. Humans try to contain God in our constructs, but God cannot be tamed.

A Grief Observed offers a glimpse at the personal struggles of C. S. Lewis in a time of sorrow. Lewis's suffering, to the extent that it is expressed here, finds little connection with the suffering of Christ, and he does not reflect on Christ's suffering. The minimal reflection on Christ shows Lewis's extreme grief. Near the end of this book, he decides to abandon his journal and reviews what he has written. He concludes that the journal displays his misplaced priorities. The journal should have focused on God and His work; instead, it was mostly about himself, then about his wife, and only at the end did it really address God.[17]

Lewis recognized the weaknesses of his journal. It was too egocentric. He realized that he did not respond as his apologetic works might suggest. What he recorded was his experience of grief. Had Lewis responded any other way, this would not be a personal account of grief but another detached, academic treatise. The compelling power, poignant emotion, and genuine character contained in this journal would have been lost. *A Grief Observed* is not a work to be used in apologetics or evangelism. It is not intended to convert or to explain the Christian faith. Instead, it reveals a human being who falls short of his expectations but relies on his faith.

CORRESPONDENCE

Throughout his life, C. S. Lewis maintained a lively correspondence with many different people. Many of these letters have been published posthumously. Some answer questions posed by the correspondent; some offer Christian encouragement; others provide insight into the personality of Lewis. They frequently reveal Lewis's theology. Letters of Christological significance will be considered according to the doctrine addressed.

IDENTITY OF CHRIST

Lewis was particularly interested in knowing the true identity of Jesus. This was so urgent because many popular ideas about Christ's identity were not biblical. For example, some people told Lewis that, in Jesus, he would find someone that he would feel compelled to love. This was not Lewis's experience. Others spoke of moral perfection, but Lewis questioned whether we really know enough of Christ's day-to-day activities to make this judgment. He thought that explanations such as those that regard Jesus simply as a good human were likely created by nineteenth-century skeptics who were denying Jesus' deity but wanted to remain Christians. This is not the picture of Jesus that emerges from the Gospels. Instead, the person who approaches the Gospels with an open mind will discover that these narratives are not given to us for our review and judgment. We are not empowered or authorized to sit in judgment over Jesus. Instead, we encounter the God who will judge us. The chief purpose of the Gospels is to introduce us to Jesus and move us to discover His identity.[18] This is vital. If

Christ's claims about Himself are not true, then He is not lovable. If, however, His claims are true, then we will react much differently.

Lewis wishes to remove illogical options about Christ, including the idea that Jesus was merely a good human teacher. In *Mere Christianity,* Lewis refutes that misconception. In his letters, he reiterates his objection that it is illogical to regard Jesus merely as a human teacher.[19] Lewis believed that such explanations of Christ's identity did not stand up to scrutiny. Jesus must be taken at His word, or He must be rejected.

Virgin Birth

Another Christological doctrine to appear in Lewis's correspondence is the virgin birth. Lewis compares and contrasts this event to ordinary experiences. Some might call Mary the bride of the Holy Spirit, but to say this is to use these words differently than we would in describing ordinary marriages. On the other hand, when we say Mary is the mother of Jesus, we are using these words in precisely the same way as we do when we describe any mother and child.[20] The second proposition is explained more clearly than the first. It is easier to describe common experiences than unique miracles. Miraculous conception is beyond normal experience, but motherhood is not. While proclaiming Mary as Jesus' mother, Lewis allowed various interpretations of the miracle. Echoing his words in *Mere Christianity* he writes,

> The exact details … an exact point at which a supernatural enters this world (whether by the creation of a new spermatozoon or the fertilisation of an ovum without a spermatozoon, or the development of a foetus without an ovum) are not part of the doctrine. These are matters in which no one is obliged and everyone is free, to speculate.[21]

Lewis is correct in noting that the specific details are not given in Scripture. However, his third possibility, the development of a fetus without an ovum, renders the true humanity of Christ suspect. Yet Lewis does not insist on any of these options, merely stating that we are free, but not bound, to speculate. He does speculate but is content to accept the miracle without such explanations.

INCARNATION

Because Lewis's understanding of Christology was focused on the incarnation, references to it are easily found in his letters. In one, Lewis and his friend Owen Barfield disagree about the meaning of Gethsemane for Christ's perfection. Lewis claimed that because Christ experienced fear, we should not be surprised by or ashamed of fear. Barfield countered that if He was afraid, He must have been imperfect. Lewis responds by comparing this to Christ's temptation. He faces all manner of temptation on behalf of humanity: from the most ordinary to those that are shockingly evil.[22] Temptation does not negate Christ's perfection. Indeed, He had to face it if He were to share humanity's plight. Whether the temptations we face are base and common or shockingly perverse, they have been faced, and conquered, by Christ. Moreover, Christ's experience was more intense than ours. This is particularly notable when we consider death. For an ordinary human, the horror of death is blunted. As frightening as it appears to be, it is simply a continuation of the fallen state that is familiar to all humanity. For Christ, however, the stakes are much higher. There is no need for Him, who possesses essential life, to die. Death is not a natural or expected occurrence for Him, and consequently, only He can truly experience the horror of death.[23]

Lewis takes his application of Gethsemane to a new level. Not only is Christ's fear in the garden related to human suffering, it is more intense. For an ordinary person to die, give in, or lose control is unpleasant, but it is not unusual. But in Christ it is perfection that submits to these things. Only He really lived a human life because only He lived perfectly. Only one who knows the fullness of life will completely know the horror of death. Fear does not nullify Christ's perfection; rather, it demonstrates it.

Finally, Lewis challenges Barfield's understanding of the incarnation. Barfield had maintained that Christ had suffered because he was a spiritual being who was shackled with a human body. Because of this, Barfield suggested that the greatest temptation of Christ was to hasten His death, discard His flesh, and return to a purely spiritual existence. Lewis aptly notes that this implies that Christ is not perfect God and perfect man but was some other type of spiritual being, trapped in a body. He flatly denies that Christ was anything less than true God. Lewis also maintains that the incarnation did not alter the full deity of Christ. Even so, the Son of God, with all His divine attributes, took on a human nature and was subject to its limitations.[24]

Lewis upholds the true deity and humanity of Christ. Christ did not suffer merely from being in the body. This gnostic understanding of the body is not in accord with the Scriptures, and it would speak against Christ's perfection. Furthermore, Lewis stressed that the incarnation does not reduce the true deity of Christ. Christ is eternally God. The incarnation did not negate His deity; if so, Lewis notes, the universe would vanish because it cannot exist apart from the presence of God and without His providence. This is a strong affirmation of His deity. Christ is eternally God, even in the incarnation. He possessed human characteristics, such as the ability to suffer, without losing His divine attributes.

Without employing the precise language of theology, Lewis is discussing the communication of attributes. The incarnation is not a reduction of the deity or an abrogation of divine attributes and functions. There never has been a time when the Second Person of the Trinity was not truly God. The incarnate Christ is fully divine and fully human.

HUMANITY

Elsewhere, Lewis discusses the humanity of Christ in more detail. This appears as he advises a nun on her translation of Athanasius's Latin treatise *On the Incarnation*. She asked whether the Latin text should be translated to say that God "became Man" or "became a man." Lewis responds that there is truth in both translations. Because the Latin text had no definite articles, either might be an appropriate translation.[25] Because of this, Lewis is able to demonstrate that the incarnation was absolutely specific. Jesus possessed human characteristics and was, in His human nature, subject to human limitations. At the same time, He became man, representative of all humanity. Lewis uses the flexibility of the Latin text to show that the one incarnate as a specific human being is the representative of all humanity. As the letter continues, Lewis addresses an apparent theological error. His correspondent had said that the Person, or the Ego, of Christ was God. Lewis questioned this statement, asserting that the human nature of Christ includes both body and soul. In saying this, Lewis affirms the orthodox doctrine of the incarnation, but he hesitates to be definitive, saying that he's not certain of his conclusion.[26] Later, another letter amplifies and strengthens Lewis's ideas. This second letter confidently says that Christ had a human body and a human soul. This complete human nature was united with the Second Person of the Trinity in the incarnation. Although this one person had a single will, He also experienced ordinary human feelings. To stress the full humanity of Christ, Lewis notes that if the divine nature had been taken away, Jesus would have been an ordinary human being, not a soulless corpse.[27]

Lewis makes several key points. The first regards the human nature of Christ. The Athanasian Creed says Christ is "Perfect God, and Perfect Man of a reasonable soul and human flesh subsisting." In the first letter, Lewis expresses the orthodox doctrine, but he qualifies his assertion. In the second letter, he is confident. If a human consists of body and soul, then the human nature of Christ must be both body and soul. To say any less is to diminish His humanity.

From this point, Lewis discusses the personal union. Christ perfectly unites deity with a human soul and body without diminishing either nature. Because He has a human nature, Christ experiences human feelings, including temptation, fear, and grief. Feelings are not inherently sinful, though some of them may become sinful if they are acted upon. Had He not experienced these feelings, He would not have been truly human. The incarnate Christ did experience our human situation, but because He was God, He did this without sinning.

CHRIST'S SUFFERING

Christ's experience of human emotions was a source of consolation and encouragement for Lewis. He frequently reminds his correspondents of Christ's experience and its significance for His people. When one woman wrote to Lewis, concerned about her feelings of fear, he answered that her lack of bravery should not disturb her. Even Christ, in Gethsemane, did not appear brave. Lewis then went on to express His gratitude for this. The struggles of Christ were a source of comfort and consolation to him in his own struggles.[28]

When a priest wrote to ask for prayer in the face of illness, Lewis agreed, but cautioned that even the strongest faith is not a guarantee against dismay. No human has a stronger faith than Christ did, but even He faced dismay in the Garden of Gethsemane.[29] Similarly, he counseled that while fear is horrible, we need not be ashamed of our fear. Even the Son of God was desperately afraid in Gethsemane. Lewis notes that he finds this fact to be comforting.[30] In each of these letters, Lewis reminds struggling Christians of the challenges faced by their Lord. Elsewhere, he relates Christ's suffering to His divine power. He clearly had the power to command whatever He wanted. Yet while praying in Gethsemane, Christ did not use this word of command, rather He made Himself reliant on His Father's will and power and not His own.[31] So it is that when His earnest request was denied, He willingly submitted to his Father's will. Christ, who is omnipotent according to His divine nature, did not use that power to escape suffering. Instead, He faced that ordeal for humanity.

This is also evident in the crucifixion. On the cross, Christ asks why God has forsaken Him. How can He be forsaken without denying the unity of the Godhead? Lewis says that the Father was not truly absent from the Son when Jesus spoke these words. Nonetheless, Jesus truly felt forsaken because He was truly human and so voluntarily submitted to this experience and these feelings.[32] Such a submission is possible only if Christ is not using His divine power. It is evidence of Christ's humiliation.

DESCENT INTO HELL

Another Christological doctrine addressed in Lewis's correspondence is the descent into hell. One letter in particular is helpful in determining Lewis's understanding of this doctrine. He says that the descent was to Hades, which he views as the place of the dead. This is distinguished from Gehenna, which Lewis calls the land of the lost. This place of the dead is outside of our human experience of time, so Christ is able to preach to the dead from all times. Lewis implies that this preaching offers some sort of a second chance, but he admits that we do not know the details. In application, he walks a middle ground. The descent reminds Christians to trust in God because He is both just and merciful. Yet Christ's descent cannot be used as an excuse for complacency in this life. It remains the duty of Christians to do everything possible to convert unbelievers.[33]

RESURRECTION

While Lewis does not claim to know all the details of the descent into hell, his belief in the resurrection of Christ is unquestioned. When a reader suggested that Christ's resurrection was simply a resurrection of His spirit not His body, Lewis answered that Luke 24 clearly proclaims that Christ rose from the dead physically.[34] Later, he would insist that a resurrection of spirit would offer no comfort. Letters with one correspondent discussed the eldila in Lewis's Space Trilogy. Lewis noted that in Scripture angels often frighten people. In contrast, the resurrected Christ frightens people only when they do not recognize the resurrection and think they are seeing a ghost.[35] He suggests two reasons why this is true. First, like us, our Lord is human. Second, a creature is closer to its creator than it is to other, superior, creatures. Because of this, Christ's followers were terrified when they believed Him to be a ghost but comforted when they saw the evidence of the bodily resurrection.

Lewis made one further application of the resurrection. Because of His resurrection and glorification, Jesus Christ did not reach old age. Lewis described his pleasure in this idea. The Lord bore many human afflictions, but He chose to remain youthful.[36] This is part of the promise of the resurrection and a glimpse of our eternal state. Christ, the archetypal man, lives in everlasting youth and vitality.

GLORIFICATION

When a young man asked Lewis about heaven, offering his own conjectures, Lewis responded with some ideas on Christ's glorification. He began by noting that it is not necessarily valid to predicate attributes to the glorified bodies of Christians that are true of the glorified body of Christ. Because He is uniquely the God-man, we cannot extrapolate information about Him from our own experience. Lewis also noted that we ought not impose restrictions on Christ because this would imply that He is somehow imperfect. As he considers the implicatons of this, however, he takes up the challenging question of presence. How is the glorified Christ, who is perfect God and perfect man, present?

All finite things have limits. This is a significant component of their identity. It is the spatial limitation of a statue that defines it. A musical note is, in part, constituted by its volume. A change in volume makes the music something different. A poem is characterized by the limitations of meter and rhyme. Might similar restrictions apply to the presence of the glorified Christ?[37] Human beings are limited to being present in one particular place at a time. God is omnipresent. What does this mean for the incarnate Christ who has both human and divine attributes? Lewis suggests that it is necessary for a perfect finite being to be locally present. For the human nature to be free of this limitation might negate its perfection. Unfortunately, Lewis does not continue the discussion. It might equally be claimed that nonlocal presence is necessary for the perfection of the divine nature. At the same time, Lewis believed that Christ was, in some way, omnipresent. He used this to comfort a woman who was worried that she might enter a nursing home, responding that Christ is present wherever she may go—even in a nursing home.[38] It would appear that he considered Christ to be omnipresent but perhaps only according to His divine nature.

The Intercession of Christ

Our Savior continues to work on our behalf, even after His ascension into heaven. Part of this ongoing work is His intercession. This view is seen as Lewis addresses the issue of charity in prayer. How does one pray for people such as Hitler or Stalin? Lewis writes that it helps if one remembers that Christ has already died for these men and is Himself interceding for them. All we do is join our voices with His.[39] The intercession, and indeed the sacrifice of Christ, apply to all people.

Atonement

One of the most interesting aspects of Lewis's correspondence is seen in letters that answer questions from his readers. One question that arises in his correspondence with Dom Bede Griffiths regards Lewis's conception of the atonement. At Lewis's request, Griffiths had critiqued *Mere Christianity*. When Griffiths objected to Lewis's treatment of the atonement, he first softened his words. Lewis had said that Christians could reject atonement theory. In this letter, Lewis says that he did not mean to state this so emphatically. Rather, he meant that it need not be used by an individual Christian who does not find such theories helpful. After correcting this overstatement, Lewis proceeds to defend his core position. He asks Griffiths to consider a different wording.

> [T]he Divinity of Our Lord *has to be believed* whether you find it a help or a "scandal" (otherwise you are not a Xtian at all) but the Anselmic theory of the Atonement is *not* in that position. Would you admit that a man was a Xtian ... who said "I believe that Christ's death redeemed man from sin, but I can make nothing of the theories as to *how*!"[40]

One must believe in the deity of Christ to be a Christian, but one does not have to subscribe to any particular theory of the atonement. Belief in the fact of the atonement is all that is required, not a particular theoretical understanding. The following year, Lewis offered an even greater concession. He said that he would not have written these things if he had suspected that theologians generally agreed with the Anselmic theory. He did not think that this theory was present in the New Testament itself nor in most of the early church fathers.[41] Griffiths had apparently convinced Lewis that the Anselmic theory was much more prevalent than he had previously assumed, yet Lewis does not concede his primary point. He might consider himself ignorant as to the frequency of this motif, but he insists that the theory itself does not have to be believed.

CONCLUSION

In his personal writings, C. S. Lewis explains his thoughts on a number of Christological doctrines, provides further explanations of his writing, and applies his faith to himself as well as to others. What emerges is a man who realizes his total dependency on God. He states this in a letter intended to comfort a woman to whom he provided financial assistance. He tells her that accepting charity reminds people that they are dependent upon others and upon God. Lewis confides that this was a difficult thing for him to learn, but it should be obvious to us. The fact that our Savior came to be crucified for us reminds us of our complete dependence on Him.[42]

It may have taken him a long time to see it, but through his personal writings, this vision becomes prominent. Lewis realizes that he owes everything to Christ.

NOTES

1. C. S. Lewis, *The Pilgrim's Regress: An Allegorical Apology for Christianity, Reason, and Romanticism* (New York: Bantam, 1933), 157.

2. Ibid., 172.

3. Ibid., 192. The "verses" that Virtue refers to are from the ancient Christian canticle *Te Deum Laudamus*, which reads, in part, "When Thou tookest upon Thee to deliver man, Thou didst humble Thyself to be born of a Virgin. When Thou hadst overcome the sharpness of death, Thou didst open the kingdom of heaven to all believers."

4. Ibid., 155.

5. Ibid., vii.

6. C. S. Lewis, *Surprised by Joy: The Shape of My Early Life* (New York: Harcourt, Brace, Jovanovich, 1955), 21.

7. Ibid., 223–24.

8. Ibid., 230.

9. Ibid., 236.

10. Ibid.

11. C. S. Lewis, *A Grief Observed* (New York: Bantam Books, 1976), 5.

12. Ibid.

13. Ibid., 33, 34.

14. Ibid., 38.

15. Ibid., 75, 76.

16. Ibid., 76.

17. Ibid., 71, 72.

18. Letter to a Lady, 26 March 1940, in *The Letters of C. S. Lewis*, W. H. Lewis (New York: Harcourt, Brace, Jovanovich, 1966), 180, 181.

19. Letter to a Lady, 8 December 1941, in *Letters of C. S. Lewis*, 196.

20. Letter to Father Peter Milward, 23 May 1951, in *Letters of C. S. Lewis*, 229.

21. Letter to a Lady, 13 June 1951, in *Letters of C. S. Lewis*, 233.

22. Letter to Owen Barfield, undated, placed between 11 August 1940 and 4 January 1941, in *Letters of C. S. Lewis*, 189.

23. Ibid., 190, 191.

24. Ibid., 191.

25. Letter to Sr. Penelope, C.S.M.V., 29 July 1942, in *Letters of C. S. Lewis*, 200, 201.

26. Ibid., 201.

27. Letter to Mrs. Frank L. Jones, [1947], in *Letters of C. S. Lewis*, 210, 211.

28. Letter to a Lady, 17 July 1953, in *Letters of C. S. Lewis*, 250.

29. Letter to the Rev. Peter Bide, 29 April 1959, in *Letters of C. S. Lewis*, 285.

30. Letter to Mary Willis Shelburne, 2 April 1955, in C. S. Lewis, *Letters to an American Lady*, ed. Clyde S. Kilby (Grand Rapids: Eerdmans, 1967), 41.

31. Letter to Don Giovanni Calabria, 25 November 1947, in Martin Moynihan trans. and ed., *The Latin Letters of C. S. Lewis* (South Bend, Ind.: St. Augustines Press, 1998), 41.

32. Letter to Mary Willis Shelburne, 20 May 1955, in *Letters to an American Lady*, 38.

33. Letter to a Lady, 31 January 1952, in *Letters of C. S. Lewis*, 238.

34. Letter to a Lady, 13 June 1951, in *Letters of C. S. Lewis*, 233.

35. Letter to Mary Willis Shelburne, 4 March 1953, in *Letters to an American Lady*, 13.

36. Letter to Don Giovanni Calabria, 19 November 1949, in *Latin Letters of C. S. Lewis*, 63.

37. Letter to "Hugh," 15 February 1961, in Lyle W. Dorsett and Marjorie Lamp Mead eds., *C. S. Lewis Letters to Children* (New York, MacMillan, 1985), 96, 97.

38. Letter to Mary Willis Shelburne, 24 November 1960, in *Letters to an American Lady*, 94.

39. Letter to Dom Bede Griffiths, 16 April 1940, in *Letters of C. S. Lewis*, 183.

40. Letter to Dom Bede Griffiths, 21 December 1941, in *Letters of C. S. Lewis*, 197, 198.

41. Letter to Dom Bede Griffiths, 13 October 1942, in *Letters of C. S. Lewis*, 201.

42. Letter to Mary Willis Shelburne, 14 June 1956, in *Letters to an American Lady*, 58.

Chapter Thirteen

Lewis, Christology, and the Creeds

Throughout his Christian writings, C. S. Lewis offers the reader a diverse and creative portrayal of the person and work of Jesus Christ. Some writings directly present his understanding; others offer a portion of his thought couched in fiction. At times Lewis precisely restates classical Christian orthodoxy but remains willing to explore new modes of expression. He clearly wanted to remain within the bounds of orthodoxy.

Was Lewis successful? To evaluate his work, we will first compare his writings to the three ecumenical creeds. Because Lewis recognized these ancient documents, they will form our primary evaluation of his theology. Following this fundamental review, we will look at two other issues. Because Lewis frequently expressed reservations about theories of the atonement, we will consider this subject in his writings. Finally, we will respond to claims that Lewis drifted into Christological heresy.

THE CREEDAL CHRISTOLOGY OF C. S. LEWIS

Lewis had no desire to be theologically innovative. Indeed, he repeatedly stated that his chief objective was to present common Christian theology. There are times when he speculates on theological topics, but he frequently concludes with creedal language, stating what "has to be believed." Because Lewis appealed to the ecumenical creeds, his writing will be compared to Christological propositions from the Apostles', Nicene, and Athanasian Creeds. These statements of universal Christian belief, based on Scripture, compose Lewis's primary theological authority.

DEITY OF CHRIST

THE ETERNALLY BEGOTTEN SON OF GOD

The creeds begin in eternity, proclaiming that Christ is the "only begotten Son of God" and that He is "begotten, not made." In *Mere Christianity*, Lewis discusses this issue, distinguishing between the begetting of the Son of God and the virgin birth. To call Christ the only begotten Son is to acknowledge that He is not a created being but truly God. Furthermore, the fact that the Son is begotten of the Father does not mean that there was a time when the Son did not exist. In *Mere Christianity*, Lewis writes that while the Son owes His nature to the Father, He is, nonetheless, begotten from all eternity. There never was a time when the Son was not begotten.[1]

This theme continues as Lewis discusses the Trinity. The Son is the Father's "self expression" and is described as "what the Father has to say."[2] These words reflect John 1, which calls Jesus the eternal Word. Lewis's words in *Miracles* also parallel this Gospel as he writes that both the Father and the Son have existed from all eternity. Neither existed before the other. The Word was with God and was God.[3] *The Problem of Pain* notes the differences between the First and Second Persons of the Trinity while maintaining the eternity of the Son,[4] and *Reflections on the Psalms* upholds this attribute of Christ, saying that He is the eternal Word.[5] Lewis clearly believed in the eternity of the Son.

OF ONE SUBSTANCE WITH THE FATHER

The Son is begotten of, but not inferior to, the Father. Christian orthodoxy asserts that He is "of one substance with the Father." While Lewis does not directly use the creedal language, he does make frequent reference to the equal deity of Christ. This is already evident in his references to the Son's eternity noted above. It is repeated in *The Problem of Pain*, where Lewis affirms the unity and coeternity of the Father and the Son.[6] The Son is fully divine and of equal Godhead with the Father.

ALL THINGS MADE BY HIM

The cosubstantiality and equality of the Son and the Father are further demonstrated in creation. Consistent with Scripture and the creeds, Lewis maintains that the Son was involved in creation. Citing the first chapters of both the Gospel according to John and the Epistle to the Colossians, Lewis says that everything, and particularly life, arose in Christ.[7] Lewis assumes the creedal doctrine and moves to a more specific point: the creation of life. The role of Christ in creation is particularly evident in Lewis's fiction. In the Chronicles of Narnia, it is not the Emperor-over-the-Sea but his son, Aslan, who creates the world.[8] Likewise, in *Out of the Silent Planet*, Maleldil the Young made and ruled the world.[9] On this subject, Lewis's fiction is clearer than his prose. The Second Person of the Trinity carries out the work of creation.

TRUE DEITY

Evidence of the deity of Christ is present throughout Lewis's writings. His fictional works demonstrate this through various Christ figures. Aslan, the creator and savior of Narnia, has divine attributes and titles. He is called Lord, he is worshiped, he forgives sins, he performs miracles, and he raises the dead. In the Space Trilogy, Maleldil creates and preserves both temporal and eternal life. He is omniscient, omnipresent, and receives the worship of his creatures. Psyche, in *Till We Have Faces,* receives the worship and honor of the crowds before they reject her, and she eventually is acknowledged among the gods. Each of these figures, which are parallel to Christ, appears to be divine.

In his nonfictional writings, Lewis strongly asserts the deity of the Christ. Attributes that are ascribed to God are also ascribed to Christ. While He was on earth, the phenomenal world, He still was God Himself, eternally in the noumenal realm.[10] Yet for Lewis, the strongest evidence for Christ's deity was His self-affirmation. Lewis's apologetic works examine the personal claims of Christ. If He is not who He claimed to be, what are the logical alternatives? Jesus could not have been merely a good moral or ethical teacher. Either He was God, as He claimed, or He was a liar or a lunatic.[11] Lewis believed in the deity of Christ and reflected that directly in his apologetic works and indirectly in his fiction.

VIRGIN BIRTH

The strongest of Lewis's Christological themes is the incarnation, which begins, in temporal terms, with the miraculous conception of Christ. *Miracles* indicates that because the virgin birth is a miracle, it was as difficult for the participants to believe as it is for any modern reader. [12] Lewis also upholds this doctrine in *Mere Christianity*. His most interesting discussion occurs in a letter in which he maintains that one can believe the miracle while speculating about the details.[13] Mary was a virgin at both the conception and birth of Jesus. Lewis states the essential teaching, then speculates in areas where he believes the doctrine is not specific. How exactly did this occur? Lewis suggests that God might have created a new spermatozoon, enabled fertilization without a spermatozoon, or developed a fetus without an ovum. While these details are not specifically a part of the doctrine, these speculations may have unintended consequences. Christ is of the same human substance as His mother. One questions how a child would be of his mother's substance apart from an ovum. Lewis's unwillingness to be dogmatic in his speculation has led him to allow for a possibility that could undermine the real humanity of Christ.

There is no doubt that Lewis believed in the virgin birth. We see reflections of this as he considers parallels in mythology. *The Discarded Image* discusses the medieval image of the unicorn. According to a medieval writer, Isidore, the only way for a hunter to kill a unicorn is to set a virgin before him. Only when the ordinarily strong unicorn lays his head in the virgin's lap and sleeps can a hunter kill it. Lewis observes that it would be hard for any Christian to ponder this rich myth without considering it as an allegory of the incarnation and crucifixion.[14] This and other parallels to Christian revelation within pagan myth caught Lewis's imagination and strengthened his belief.

OF HIS MOTHER'S SUBSTANCE

Concerns arising from Lewis's imprecision regarding the nature of the virgin birth fade when the next article of the creeds is introduced. According to His human nature, Christ is of the substance of His mother. Lewis affirms this in *Mere Christianity* when he writes that Christ's human nature (which Lewis refers to as His "created life," or "natural human creature") was derived from his mother.[15] In *Reflections on the Psalms*, Lewis reminds the reader that in the incarnation, Jesus submitted Himself to a specific human heredity and to the cultural environment of a particular people.[16] He received this heredity and learned of this culture from Mary, who was a mother to Jesus in the same sense as any other human mother.[17] After speculating on the details of the virgin birth, Lewis returns to a restatement of creedal doctrine. Jesus was fully human, of Mary's substance.

REASONABLE SOUL AND HUMAN FLESH

The creeds are additionally concerned with the nature of Jesus' humanity. The Athanasian Creed states that He is "Perfect God, and Perfect Man of a reasonable soul and human flesh subsisting." In *Letters to Malcolm*, Lewis says that the Son of God has taken a human body and soul into Himself. In so doing, He took on all that it means to be human.[18] When Athanasius's treatise *On the Incarnation* was translated to say that the Person, or Ego, of Christ was God, Lewis responded that he thought a human soul was involved because Christ's humanity involved more than His body.[19] He confidently restates this in a letter, saying that a complete human nature, both body and soul, was brought together in a personal union with the Second Person of the Trinity.[20] Lewis maintained that Christ was fully human; therefore, He must have had a human soul.

While Lewis stresses Christ's deity, His full humanity also remains evident in Lewis's writings. One of the most dramatic references is in *Mere Christianity* where Lewis makes the incarnation as specific as possible. Christ assumed a human nature with particular human characteristics: a specific height, weight, and hair color. He lived among a specific people group and spoke their language.[21]

God, who created humans with bodies, assumed a human body as His own. This is emphasized in *The Pilgrim's Regress* where we read that the "Landlord's Son" was not ashamed to be in the body.[22] When a friend suggested that Christ suffered because He was in the body and, therefore, was tempted to hasten His own death, Lewis responded that this would deny that Christ is perfect God and perfect man.[23] The body is not a burden, but it is part of the human nature of Christ.

Not only is Christ truly human, He is exceptionally human. Jesus Christ is the archetypal man. Lewis sees a strong reflection of this in Christ's use of the title "Son of Man." He understands this designation to mean the archetypal man—the one who comes not only to redeem humanity, but to ennoble it.[24] The resurrection and ascension are not merely great acts of God, but they also are the triumph of man. Christ again appears as the archetypal man in *Mere Christianity*. He is *the* new man, the pattern of the redeemed and recreated humanity.[25] Even the humanity of Christ is something greater than might have been expected.

The true humanity of Christ is demonstrated as He faces a variety of human situations and responds appropriately. The greatest example of this, for Lewis, was in Gethsemane. Christ's struggles before His death demonstrate His humanity. For example, in *Letters to Malcolm*, Lewis writes that without this struggle to escape torment, it would have seemed that Christ was not truly human.[26]

SIGNIFICANCE OF THE INCARNATION

Clearly, Lewis held to the reality of the incarnation, viewing it with awe. Throughout his writings, he upholds its significance. For example, the Space Trilogy presents a variety of sentient life forms on Malacandra, which was created before the incarnation, but on Perelandra, the sentient beings are humanoid. How could they take any other form once Maleldil had become a man? The incarnation also changed humanity's perception of God. In *That Hideous Strength*, Ransom notes that Maleldil once was frightening, as are the *eldila*, but the incarnation has changed this perspective.[27] That same idea is expressed in *The Screwtape Letters* where the demons call the incarnation one of God's advantages.[28]

Lewis was particularly interested in the incarnation as it was prefigured in pagan mythology. He explicitly deals with the Corn-king myths and alludes to other mythical figures, such as Osiris, Balder, and Adonis. After observing the pattern in other mythology, a crucial step in Lewis's own conversion was the realization that, in Christ alone, the pattern of these myths has become reality. In Christ, God really has become human.[29] Yet the incarnation is beyond our expectations. It is the great iconoclast, shattering our human conceptions of the Messiah.[30] The incarnation is a unique event foreseen in nature and throughout the world, and it is of paramount importance for the Christian.

The Personal Union of Christ

The challenges of Christology become evident when the interaction of the human and divine natures of Christ is considered. In *Miracles,* Lewis compares the union of the eternal *logos* with a human organism to the union of reason and flesh in one person. In *Mere Christianity,* he speaks of the human and divine natures being amalgamated together. While these explanations, particularly that of amalgamation, may be misleading, the desire to show the union of the two natures is evident.

Communication of Attributes

Lewis's writings affirm that a human and divine nature were united in one Christ. For example, in *Miracles* he identifies the incarnate Christ with Yahweh[31] and compares Christianity to the Corn-king myths. Yahweh does not die and rise each year as a true Corn-king should, but He does die and rise once. Although mortality is a human attribute, because of the incarnation, Lewis ascribes it also to the divine nature. Yahweh died, not merely the human Jesus. Likewise, in the resurrection both natures rose, not merely the divine.[32] Late in his life, Lewis demonstrated his belief that this personal union extends beyond the ascension as well, complaining that Christians frequently fail to emphasize and rejoice in the eternal, glorified humanity of Christ. He will never abandon this human nature.

The incarnation is not merely a temporary state. Throughout his writings, Lewis stresses the enduring character of this miracle. Christ's humanity is never to be abandoned. Likewise, in *Mere Christianity,* Lewis reminds his readers that Christ is not simply a man who once lived on earth. He *is* still human—just as human as He was during His ministry on earth. He also remains fully God—as He has been for all eternity.[33] The same theme is present in Lewis's fictional writings. In *The Screwtape Letters*, the demons say that Christ is still clothed in human flesh.[34] That form, in Lewis's thinking, is eternally young and vital. Despite the taunts of mockers who say that He must be old, Aslan does not appear to age. Instead, he is perpetually young and strong. In *That Hideous Strength*, Ransom appears to be a young man. At the end of the story, he is taken to live immortally on Perelandra until the end of the worlds. The perpetual youth of Christ was a source of strength for Lewis, who wrote in a letter that Christ, the archetypal man, is eternally young.[35] The Christ remains human, but He is glorified, and, therefore, He does not age.

Lewis believed the attributes of the human nature were shared with the divine nature in the incarnation. Is the reverse true as well? Are divine attributes communicated to the human nature? While he never fully addresses this question, Lewis does address several attributes. One is omnipresence. God is able to be universally present, but human nature is limited by finite space. How are these two paradoxical states resolved? In a 1961 letter, Lewis suggests that the perfection of a finite creature may demand a local presence. If Christ was perfectly human, does this not necessitate that He be finite? However, Lewis ends by qualifying his comments, saying that he is only guessing about these things.[36]

A similar concern arises with the issue of divine knowledge. Lewis considers divine omniscience in relation to the incarnation. While historic Christianity has maintained that Christ was perfect and without error, Lewis was willing to consider the possibility that Christ, in His earthly ministry, may have made scientific or historical errors. He ascribes such possible errors to Christ's humanity, explaining that he did not think that Christ, in the flesh, was omniscient. The finite human brain cannot contain unlimited knowledge. Therefore, to ascribe omniscience to the human Christ would be a denial of the incarnation. This would, in effect, result in the heresy called Docetism.[37] Here, as with omnipresence, Lewis restricts the availability of the divine attributes. While a later edition of *The Problem of Pain* downplays this statement, Lewis continues to limit the human nature of Christ.

UNION NOT BY CONVERSION OF GODHEAD INTO FLESH BUT BY TAKING MANHOOD INTO GOD

While Lewis does not ascribe all the divine attributes to the incarnate Christ, he does not consider the incarnation to be a reduction of the divine nature. In this, he follows the Athanasian Creed, which says that Christ is one "not by conversion of the Godhead into flesh but by taking of the Manhood into God." Lewis cites this formula to describe the incarnation in *Reflections on the Psalms*, commenting that the human flesh thus bears divine life.[38] Again in *Mere Christianity*, Lewis states that Christ's natural human nature was completely taken up into the divine nature.[39] Finally, in *Letters to Malcolm*, Lewis writes that the Second Person of the Trinity has taken the human body and soul into Himself. Along with that nature, Christ took up everything that humans are and everything that we face.[40] Lewis repeatedly quotes or paraphrases these words from the creed because their point is critical to his understanding of the incarnation. Deity is not diminished by the incarnation—humanity is ennobled. Humanity becomes what it was intended to be and what it one day will be, in Christ.

THE WORK OF CHRIST

SUFFERED UNDER PILATE

As Lewis follows the basic creedal doctrines regarding the person of Christ, so he continues to do this regarding the work of Christ. As the creeds say that Christ suffered under Pontius Pilate, so Lewis cites the role of Pilate to demonstrate the historicity of the biblical account.[41] Lewis also strongly emphasizes Christ's suffering. Throughout his writings, he notes that Christ suffered, that He is preeminent for suffering, and that He was tortured to death.[42]

This emphasis is most pronounced in Lewis's later writings. After witnessing the suffering of his wife, Lewis focused more on the suffering of Christ. He would write in *Letters to Malcolm* that the suffering of Christ reflected the human situation of suffering and rejection. He would also write about how the horror of the crucifixion must periodically be faced.[43] In *The Four Loves*, Lewis discusses the boundless love of Christ that causes Him to create the universe though He foresees His own suffering.[44] While the passion of Christ is mentioned in earlier books and presented in Lewis's fictional works, it is most poignant in his later writings.

DEATH

The creeds simply declare that Christ died. Lewis's writings, likewise, note the death of Christ with simplicity. In *Miracles*, he denies an anthropocentrism that makes humans the center of all creation. This is not the essence of Christianity. Instead, the heart of the Christian faith is the belief that God, motivated by His love for humanity, became a man and died.[45] Christ's principal work was to suffer and be killed.[46] He is the perfect man and, therefore, the only one who could perfectly die on behalf of all humanity.[47] His death is foreseen from the foundation of the world,[48] is foretold through prophecy, and is reflected in the dying god myths.[49]

Likewise, the death of Christ is prevalent in Lewis's fiction. Aslan dies on the Stone Table for Edmund's treachery. Maleldil wrestles with the Bent One on Thulcandra to become a ransom. Elwin Ransom battles the Un-man on Perelandra to end his temptation of that planet. Psyche becomes the Accursed, sacrificed on a tree for her nation. The most ironic reference to the death of Christ is spoken by a damned bishop who considered the death to be a tragic waste.[50] In satirizing the bishop, Lewis shows the deep meaning of Christ's death.

BURIAL

Following His death on the cross, Christ was buried. Surprisingly, Lewis does not specifically mention this simple detail. He writes of the death and resurrection, but he never mentions Christ's burial. The closest reference comes with the death of Aslan. Susan and Lucy care for the lion's body as the women cared for Jesus' body, but in this case they do not remove it from the Stone Table. Aslan is restored to life without being buried. In all other contexts, Lewis simply assumes that Jesus was buried.

DESCENT INTO HELL

Among the more disputed Christological doctrines is the descent into hell. Based primarily upon 1 Peter 3:18–20, it is simply stated in the Apostles' and Athanasian Creeds that "He descended into hell." Despite this paucity of information, Lewis makes significant use of the descent. Before his conversion to Christianity, he published a series of poems entitled *Spirits in Bondage*. The original title was *Spirits in Prison*, alluding to 1 Peter 3. Although the poems do not discuss the work of Christ, the reference is significant for the atheistic Lewis. Following his conversion, Lewis made more use of this theme. On Perelandra, Ransom kills the demonic Un-man in a subterranean cavern before his "resurrection" to the planet's surface. In *Till We Have Faces*, Psyche is sent on a journey through the Underworld to acquire from death a casket of beauty to give to Orual. In *Miracles*, Lewis

174

describes the incarnation and ministry of Christ in terms of a diver who descends to the depths to recover a valuable object. He finds it when he descends deep into the water where life is no longer evident.[51] While all of these stories draw upon the imagery of the descent into hell, they do not adequately reveal Lewis's understanding of the descent.

Elsewhere, however, Lewis does provide his interpretation of the descent. In a 1952 letter, he wrote that the descent was to Hades, the abode of all the dead, not to Gehenna, which Lewis describes as the land of the lost. The descent took place outside of time, thus it could include people who lived before and after Christ's earthly ministry. In this letter, Lewis does not offer an interpretation of what happened. Nonetheless, Lewis is confident that God will treat people with both justice and mercy. Furthermore, because of the possibility of damnation, it remains our responsibility to do everything in our power to bring God's Word to others.[52]

Lewis considers the descent to be for the sake of those who had never heard of Christ. Thus, the descent provides for the spread of salvation. This restates the argument of *The Great Divorce*. Here Lewis maintains that the descent took place outside of time. Because of this, every person in hell—past, present, and future—was there when Christ descended. He went to preach to them all.[53] The descent is into hell, but it is hell before the final judgment. Some hear and presumably are saved by Christ's preaching. This is reflected in the narrative as a ghost from hell is able to enter heaven. Lewis portrays Christ's descent into hell as the offer of salvation, outside of time, to those who have or will have died. It is not to suffer the punishment for sins but to proclaim the possibility of salvation.

RESURRECTION

Lewis strongly believed in the physical resurrection of Jesus Christ and incorporated it on many levels into his writings. He reminds his readers that the earliest Christians were converted by a single fact, the resurrection.[54] It was not merely a resurrection of the soul, but of the body,[55] a resurrection foretold by Christ.[56] Both natures of Christ were united in the resurrection, so it was not only the divine, but also the human, who rose.[57]

Lewis's fiction also contains resurrection images. Aslan is alive and whole following his sacrifice. Psyche is seen alive after the Great Offering. Ransom also is alive and well after his victory on Perelandra. Lewis's illustrations of the work of Christ in *Miracles* further portray the resurrection. The strongman who stoops to pick up an enormous load emerges victorious; the diver who plunges to the depths of the sea returns with the object that he sought. Christ's victory changes everything; it displays his power, glory, and triumph. The Savior has fought a battle against death itself. This enemy, which had reigned since humanity's fall into sin, has finally been vanquished.[58]

ASCENSION

The ascension of Christ is also an important doctrine for Lewis. In *Miracles*, he repeatedly answers the objection that Christianity seems to be based on an antiquated worldview. This is particularly true as Lewis discusses the ascension because some might envision a heaven beyond the clouds where Jesus sits on a gold throne at the right of His Father. Faced with this simplistic understanding, Lewis considers the possibility that Christians could simply reject this teaching. He replies that this may only be done if the post-resurrection appearances of Christ are the appearances of a ghost or are hallucinations. These things might fade away, but if Christ really had been raised from the dead, He has a genuine human body. That body could not simply disappear, it had to go somewhere.[59] Lewis continues to state that if the ascension is denied, either the physical resurrection must be denied or another explanation must be offered to explain Christ's missing body. Lacking such an explanation, Lewis holds to the resurrection and ascension.

In a 1942 sermon on miracles, Lewis said that we have no good reason to classify the ascension as an allegory because it is presented to us as a literal event. Lewis went on to speculate that Christ withdrew from this dimension to worlds beyond human experience. He compares this possibility to modern physics, which proposes a variety of ideas beyond observable experience. If hypotheses such as these may be entertained by the modern mind, Lewis proposed that it is not irrational to think that Christ left the three-dimensional space that we perceive with our senses yet still existed in His body. Perhaps this means that He has access to higher dimensions of space and sense that we cannot directly experience.[60]

While he does not insist on this interpretation of the ascension, Lewis maintains that it makes the doctrine more logical to the modern reader while upholding the integrity of the biblical account.

SITS AT THE RIGHT HAND OF GOD

The creeds state that following His ascension, Christ sits at the right hand of God the Father in heaven. In discussing the ascension, Lewis rejected the crass image of two chairs placed side by side. In *The Great Divorce*, he paraphrases the messianic Psalm 110. Where the psalmist writes, "Sit at My right hand until I make Your enemies a footstool for Your feet" (110:1), Lewis describes what this means. In his paraphrase, the master is invited to share His Master's rest and splendor. His enemies would be vanquished, and He would be given eternal authority, power, and strength.[61] As this paraphrase continues, Lewis writes of authority, power, and strength being given to Christ forever. Lewis thus removes spatial considerations and focuses on perpetual power and honor.

CHRIST'S RETURN FOR JUDGMENT AND HIS ETERNAL KINGDOM

Lewis's writings consistently hold to the return of Christ for judgment and His eternal reign. Lewis noted that these teachings have been part of the Christian faith as it has been understood everywhere and by everyone.[62] His essay "The World's Last Night" begins by quoting the Apostles' Creed and various Bible passages that address Christ's return, remarking that these passages make it evident that the doctrine of Christ's return is a fundamental part of historic Christianity.[63] Still, there is considerable anxiety among Christians regarding teachings of the end times. Lewis notes that many people are apprehensive because they are reacting to those who would see this doctrine as Christ's central message.[64]

Lewis denied that this doctrine was Christ's essential teaching, but he maintained that it is an integral part of the faith and so must be accepted. Lewis believed that Christ clearly taught that He would return, but there is no way for us to determine exactly when this return will occur. In light of this, we are to be prepared to meet Christ whenever He comes.[65] Readiness is vital because the return of Christ will be for judgment. When He returns, no time will remain to prepare for Him. Either we will welcome Him with joy, or we will be horrified that we rejected our Savior.[66]

Lewis's general approach to Christ's return thus stresses preparation. The return itself will be marked by judgment. Responding to those who would try to reject this teaching, Lewis demonstrates that there is no way to ignore this theme because it is so clearly a part of Christ's own words. Lewis cites a number of Bible passages in evidence of this, including the separation of the sheep and the goats (Matthew 25:31–46), the narrow path (Matthew 7:13–14), the wheat and the tares (Matthew 13:24–30), the 10 virgins (Matthew 25:1–13), and the parable of the net (Matthew 13:47–50).[67] Christians teach these things because Christ taught them.

The theme of judgment also finds a place in Lewis's fiction. At the end of *The Last Battle*, Aslan judges all creatures at the end of the world. Some enter paradise; others disappear into his shadow. In *The Great Divorce*, the souls in the grey city are aware that it is twilight and true night and darkness are coming. *The Screwtape Letters* candidly depicts the salvation or damnation of souls. Lewis certainly maintained that Christ's return would be marked with judgment. But this is not a burden for believers. While his depiction of judgment includes damnation, the chief focus is on paradise. Some may pass into Aslan's shadow, but the story focuses on the redeemed. Souls may return to the grey city, but the reality of heaven is greater and more substantial. Christ's judgment ends with His joyful and eternal reign.

LEWIS AND THE CREEDS

Overall, C. S. Lewis presents a Christology that is consistent with the creeds that he regularly confessed in worship. He often states doctrines directly from these statements of belief and frequently explains and illustrates them. When his explanations of certain doctrines go beyond the propositions of the creeds, he is more likely to present a theology at variance with different Christian groups. This is particularly evident in his treatment of the virgin birth, the communication of attributes between Christ's two natures, and the descent into hell. While he occasionally uses imprecise language or speculation, Lewis returns to the essential language and content of the creeds. Because of this, the Christ presented in both fictional and nonfictional contexts is largely consistent with historic orthodoxy.

ATONEMENT THEORY

While Lewis's broad categories of Christology are anchored in the creeds, his greatest personal challenge in Christology regarded theories of the atonement. Throughout the history of the Christian church, different theologians have explained the atonement and organized the doctrines that compose it through the use of specific "theories." Lewis claimed to avoid these explanations, yet he eclectically incorporated elements from various theories into his own writings.

One theory, however, finds no significant use in his writing. The Abelardian theory of the atonement considers Christ's work primarily as an example to humanity. While Lewis frequently views Christ as an example, he is unwilling to reduce Christ's work to that simple perspective. Other atonement theories are more complex.

Lewis objects to a particularly narrow expression of the Anselmic theory of the atonement (a theory also known as the vicarious satisfaction, substitutionary atonement, or Latin theory of the atonement). According to Lewis's understanding of this theory, humanity rejected God and fell under His wrath. He wanted to punish us, but Christ chose to be punished in our stead. Because the punishment had been paid, God forgave us.[68] His words against the atonement theory are directed against this explanation.

Lewis has three fundamental objections to such theories of the atonement. First, he did not find the explanations helpful. They did not answer all his questions and seemed too simple. Second, he was troubled with the logic of the Anselmic theory as he understood it. If God was going to forgive sin apart from merit, why did He not simply forgive? Was it truly necessary for such a drastic step to be taken? In response, Lewis came to understand that as long as humanity had free will, God would have to repeat this forgiveness infinitely. This answer did not dispel Lewis's questions. Similar to this objection was the question of justice. What is the point in punishing an innocent person? God is just in punishing sin, but is it just to punish one who never sinned? Lewis's third objection was pragmatic. When he first became a Christian, he thought that one had to accept the Anselmic theory. He eventually came to the conclusion that the explanation is not Christianity, but it is a proposed explanation of how Christianity works. A person can be a Christian without holding any specific theory of the atonement. In fact, there really is no way that a believer would understand this work until he has accepted it.[69] Lewis clarifies his objections in a letter in which he wrote that he overstated his position. He had meant to say that a Christian was not required to use atonement theories if they were unhelpful, rather than to say that a Christian should reject such theories. Yet Lewis insisted that atonement theories themselves are not the Christian faith; rather, they are an explanation of Christianity.[70]

There is little doubt that Lewis was influenced by Gustaf Aulén's 1931 book *Christus Victor*, which was in Lewis's personal library at the time of his death. Aulén argued that legal theories of the atonement, such as the Anselmic theory, did not become prominent until the Middle Ages. Before that time, and particularly in the patristic era, the prevailing understanding of the work of Christ was as victory. This victory was frequently described as liberty for captives, which had been secured by the payment of ransom to a captor. Seen in such a form, Christ's death is payment, or ransom, made to the devil, thereby gaining freedom for humanity. Yet in taking the ransom, the captor is defeated. Pope Gregory the Great compared this to a baited hook. Christ's humanity and mortality were the "bait" that attracted the devil, who was then "hooked" by the deity of Christ. When the ransom is paid, ruin is brought upon the captor. Themes of victory and ransom, as well as the financial models of payment that make up this theory, are prevalent in Lewis's writings.

Examination of Lewis's writings shows that he really objected only to a narrow expression of the Anselmic theory. Yet he was also able to write that Christians are free to describe the death of Christ in a variety of ways. One may say that the Father forgives us because our Lord has done something for us that we should have done. Some may prefer to say that we are washed in the blood of the Lamb and, therefore, redeemed. Christ's work may be described as the defeat of death. These are not mutually exclusive descriptions. All are truthful summations of His work.[71]

This mixing of themes is Lewis's ultimate view of the atonement. He offers a rich expression that draws on diverse models.

The *Christus Victor* Model

There was much in the *Christus Victor* description of the atonement that appealed to Lewis. It was filled with rich themes that appealed to his love of mythology. Strong motifs of warfare and victory over evil were compelling in time of war. Themes of Christ vanquishing Satan to free humanity fill Lewis's writings. In *Miracles*, he describes the Lord as a powerful warrior who fights and conquers the king of death.[72]

Similar images are scattered throughout his writings, but are most evident in his fiction. In *Perelandra*, for example, Ransom physically fights and kills the Un-man in a subterranean cavern, finally casting his body into a pit of fire. It is with physical strength, below the surface of the planet, that evil is destroyed. Aslan also displays elements of the Victor theory, though simultaneously offering elements of the Anselmic theory. Aslan dies as a substitute for Edmund, but this pays a debt not to the emperor, but to the White Witch as a ransom. Following his resurrection, Aslan proceeds to the witch's castle, where he breaks down the gates and restores to life those whom the witch had turned to stone. The destruction of the castle gates is particularly reflective of the medieval images of the harrowing of hell, which described Christ's destruction of the gates of hell to lead the prisoners forth to life. Aslan then leads his newly quickened followers into battle, where the witch is killed and her magic destroyed. The parallels to the *Christus Victor* motif are numerous. After accepting the ransom, the evil one finds that she has been undone and is vanquished.

When one includes the paying of a ransom to the captor, the victory theme becomes even more obvious. Aslan conquers the White Witch, but first he offers payment to her for the crimes of Edmund. He is the ransom for the captive child. Likewise, when Ransom is wrestling with his role as savior of Perelandra, he hears the voice of God saying that He is also a Ransom. Elwin Ransom was called by that God to serve this world and help prevent its fall into sin. Yet if he did not succeed, Maleldil would not abandon this planet. If necessary, this world would also be redeemed by a gracious act of God.[73]

In his nonfictional writing, Lewis also considers the atonement in terms of paying a debt or ransom. While he objects that the Anselmic theory is unjust when it punishes an innocent person, Lewis uses this theory and clarifies it. There is no point in punishing an innocent person for a criminal offense, but this is not unusual when put in financial terms. One can pay another's debt. The same motif is seen as Lewis discusses Psalm 49. Humanity's salvation comes at too high a price for anyone to pay except the Son of God. His crucifixion paid that debt for all people.[74] Because Lewis envisions the ransom being paid not to God, but to the devil, this is an expression of the *Christus Victor* theory.

THE ANSELMIC THEORY

Despite Lewis's favoring of the *Christus Victor* model and his criticisms of the Anselmic theory, elements of the latter are found in his writings. The redemption of Aslan is primarily presented as one of victory. Yet Aslan dies in the place of Edmund, clearly a vicarious death. Likewise, Ransom fights to victory over evil, but he is not from that world. He was transported to Perelandra to fight evil. While he was involved in mortal combat, the inhabitants of Perelandra did not have to face that trial. Ransom was their substitute. Psyche faces death in the Great Offering to free the land from its drought. In this, she was the substitute for all Glome. All these fictional images of Christ involve substitution—a notable component of the Anselmic theory.

In his nonfictional writings, Lewis also describes the substitutionary death of Christ. In *Miracles*, he describes Christ's death using language that is remarkably similar to the Anselmic theory. He writes that the Redeemer had to voluntarily become man and had to be perfect. He would undergo a perfect death to defeat death or redeem death. Christ dies in the place of all others, giving us the benefits of that innocent death.[75] The only essential element of the Anselmic theory missing from this passage is that the "payment" is made to God. For all his objections to this theory, it is remarkable to see how much Lewis reverts to its basic principles.

In 1942, Lewis wrote again to Dom Bede Griffiths about the Anselmic theory. In this letter, Lewis explains that he would not have said the things he did if he had thought that there was considerable agreement among theologians on the truth of the Anselmic theory. He said that he did not believe that it was explicitly taught by the New Testament or by the majority of the early church fathers.[76] While the degree of consensus on this theory of the atonement is uncertain, it is significant that Lewis was willing to concede his ignorance if the majority of theologians were against him. If he was in error, Lewis was willing to admit his mistake and seek correction.

Lewis was partially in error. His arguments against the Anselmic theory seem somewhat inconsistent when compared to his own presentation of the atonement. It is surprising that Lewis, who sought explanation and clarity in other areas of theology, did not use these tools to explain Christ's work. Nevertheless, his key point remains correct. Theories of the atonement may be helpful, but they are not, in themselves, essential. For the believer, the most important thing is not exactly *how* Christ's death saves us but that it *does*.

CHRISTOLOGICAL HERESIES

Discussion of Christology, as of theology in general, involves not only a positive expression of doctrine, but also the avoidance of heresy. Some critics of C. S. Lewis have accused him of heresy. One of the most direct of these critics was the American theologian Norman Pittenger, who published an article criticizing Lewis's Christology. Pittenger charged that Lewis's depiction of Christ reflects Docetism and Gnosticism and that it presents the ancient heresies of Apollinarianism and Eutychianism.[77] Lewis responded to other criticisms in Pittenger's article but did not respond directly to the allegations of Christological heresy. In general, Pittenger, along with other critics, claimed that Lewis's Christology is focused strongly on Jesus' deity while neglecting His humanity.

Lewis certainly did not consider his theology heretical. Indeed, his explicit goal was to restate orthodox teaching in a fresh manner. Yet he was not formally trained in theology and used novel and sometimes imprecise language. Moreover, much of his doctrinal thought is expressed in myth and narrative. It is difficult to exercise the precision necessary in theology within these genres while avoiding allegory. A perfect parallel might have doc-

183

trinal precision, but if allegorization is avoided, a writer may more readily be accused of heresy. Lewis's writing allows for broad interpretation—a characteristic that may cause some to find heresy where it was not intended. Even so, the charges are significant and should be considered.

DOCETISM

Docetism is the teaching that Christ only *appeared* to have a human body. This notion is related to Gnosticism, which maintains, in part, that matter is evil and thus incompatible with the transcendent goodness of God, who is pure spirit. If matter is evil, God could not truly become incarnate in a material body but could only appear human. It is true that Lewis strongly emphasizes the deity of Christ, but he certainly was not a Docetist, nor does an emphasis on Christ's divinity make him a gnostic. Indeed, one would have to ignore the significant incarnational themes throughout Lewis's writings to construe him as a Docetist. In *The Problem of Pain*, Lewis suggests that Christ was not omniscient in the flesh because a finite human brain could not contain unlimited knowledge. He goes on to say that if we do not account for the limitations of His human brain, we may actually deny the incarnation and teach Docetism.[78] Clearly, Lewis was aware of Docetism and sought to avoid it. His recurring themes of the real suffering of Christ and His connection to humanity argue against Docetism. Lewis's fiction also emphasizes the incarnation—a teaching that is antithetical to Docetism. Aslan is true beast and repeatedly described in terms of his "animalness." In the Space Trilogy, sentient life on Perelandra is humanoid because Maleldil had become incarnate. Moreover, Lewis stresses the physical suffering and death of Christ. The resurrected Christ is not spirit only, but also flesh. Lewis's explanation of the ascension again demonstrates his belief that Christ was truly incarnate in human flesh and remains in that body. These writings refute the charge of Docetism.

APOLLINARIANISM

Pittenger also charges that Lewis's Christology is Apollinarian, a heresy that claims that the human mind of Christ was replaced by the divine mind. This charge, likewise, fails when

Lewis's writings are examined. His focus on the prayer of Christ in Gethsemane demonstrates the human mind and will of Christ. Echoing the language of the Athanasian Creed, Lewis repeatedly states that the incarnation involved a human body and soul. Christ was fully human. Lewis even stated that if the divine Son had been removed from Christ, what would remain would not be a corpse but a living human being. These statements are irreconcilable with Apollinarianism.

EUTYCHIANISM

The charge that Lewis tends toward Eutychianism has more substance. Lewis's desire to show that Christ was both God and man led him to call Christ a "composite" being and to speak of the human nature being "amalgamated" with the divine nature. This language could easily lead one to suspect a mixture of the two natures to produce a unique third nature. Lewis also uses the analogy of the union of "supernatural" reason and flesh to make one person. He virtually insists that this analogy be used, saying that without it, the personal union would be a fatal stumbling block. Because most people do not consider themselves to have two separate natures, this could lead to a confusion of Christ's two natures. But Lewis qualifies his statements, noting that there really is no way for ordinary humans to understand the consciousness of the divine Christ. He considers the union to be above human understanding and a mystery. It is doubtful that Lewis held to a Eutychian Christology, yet his imprecise language may lead some to that conclusion.

MODALISM

One further heresy that must be considered is Modalism. Modalism is a trinitarian heresy that teaches that God is one person who reveals Himself in different modes or expressions. This may be illustrated as God wearing three different masks. It is the same person behind each mask, but He is perceived in a different manner. Lewis did not advocate a modalistic Trinity, yet his work has been said to have modalistic inclinations. Hence, a brief examination of Lewis's trinitarian understanding is in order.

In his nonfiction works, Lewis spends considerable time explaining the Trinity, at times using questionable descriptions.

Most significant here is *The Problem of Pain*, in which Lewis discusses submission. He notes that the Son submits to the Father, but in his description, Lewis refers to God *as* Father and God *as* Son. The immediate context seems to indicate that Lewis is stressing the unity of God, but the method of description may evoke images of one person changing roles. While submission infers a plurality, Lewis's description may unintentionally stress the unity to the detriment of the Trinity.

In *Mere Christianity*, Lewis considers the development of the doctrine of the Trinity in early Christianity. This, he says, is the origin of theology. Believers had already known about God, though their knowledge was incomplete and even vague. Then they encountered Jesus, who said that He was God. His claims were compelling—all the more when considered in light of His resurrection. Then, when believers had been formed into the church, they again experienced God, this time within the church. When they had brought these truths together, they arrived at the doctrine of the Trinity.[79]

Preconceptions will be particularly evident in the interpretation of this passage. If the reader assumes the doctrine of the Trinity, he will see it in this passage, yet the lack of names may lead some to suspect modalism. After writing these words, however, Lewis reverts to more typical language, comparing the Trinity to a cube. As a cube is one shape but consists of six conjoined squares, so God consists of three persons but remains one God.[80] Lewis did hold to the doctrine of the Trinity, though his discussion tends to confuse the distinction between the three persons.

The doctrine of the Trinity becomes somewhat more problematic in Lewis's fiction. Any presentation of the doctrine of the Trinity requires a degree of precision that is difficult to attain in a fictional work without resorting to allegory. Thus, it is not surprising to find uncertain trinitarian images in his fiction. This is particularly true in the Chronicles of Narnia, in which Lewis obviously offers Christian allusions yet writes for children. Aslan clearly is a Christ figure, dying and rising again to forgive the sins of others, but he is also seen creating the world and giving faith. In *The Voyage of the Dawn Treader*, Aslan appears as an albatross and gives encouragement. Aslan thus seems to fulfill the roles not only of Christ, but of the Father and Spirit as well. At the same time, Aslan is the son of the Emperor-over-the-Sea. This emperor is also depicted as God, but he is utterly transcendent and completely unknown. His is the deep magic that necessitates the death of Aslan, and his magic cannot be changed. The godhead in Narnia is focused almost entirely upon Aslan, which indeed appears modalistic. The imprecision of Narnia may be partially explained by considering the intended readers. The Space Trilogy, on the other hand, was written for adults. In this series, God is referred to as Maleldil. The Redeemer is, properly, Maleldil the Young, though most often is simply called Maleldil. There is some passing reference to "the Old One" and a cryptic reference to "the Third One," but most references to the divine are simply to Maleldil.

Overall, though Lewis uses the language of the Trinity, his writings are focused on the incarnate Christ. Lewis's theology is wonderfully Christ-centered. The reader may, however, be left with a vagueness concerning the Father and the Holy Spirit, likely because the vagueness was Lewis's own. In the end, it appears that Lewis believed that if one knew Christ, he would know the Father and the Spirit also.

Are Lewis's writings heretical? While his imprecise language may leave questions in the minds of some readers, he clearly intended to express orthodox theology. It is also significant to note that if Lewis erred, he was not persistent in error but sought correction. He frequently sought the reaction and advice of others before publishing his writing. For example, before publishing *Mere Christianity*, he sent it to four clergymen for their critiques. Even with that, there were times when his expression of doctrine fell short of the orthodoxy to which he aspired. But in these times, he was an errorist willing to be corrected, not a heretic.

CONCLUSION

C. S. Lewis presents his Christology in a variety of different forms, from direct discourse to fictional accounts. His stated intent is to present orthodox theology in new patterns. This he does, often repeating or paraphrasing the wording of the creeds as that which "has to be believed." While he repeatedly speculates on topics that he considers open questions, he typically returns to the core beliefs of the ecumenical creeds. His writings have included nearly all the creedal material directly and all of it indirectly. At times Lewis's Christology lacks doctrinal precision, though this is an understandable fault that is easily attributable to his lack of formal theological training. This layman admirably translates mere Christianity to a wide audience.

NOTES

1. C. S. Lewis, *Mere Christianity* (New York: Macmillan, 1952), 149–50.
2. Ibid., 151.
3. C. S. Lewis, *Miracles* (New York: Macmillan, 1947), 73, 76.
4. C. S. Lewis, *The Problem of Pain* (New York: Macmillan, 1962), 90–91.
5. C. S. Lewis, *Reflections on the Psalms* (New York: Harcourt, Brace, Jovanovich, 1958), 134.
6. Lewis, *Problem of Pain*, 45.
7. Lewis, *Miracles*, 76.
8. C. S. Lewis, *The Magician's Nephew* (New York, MacMillan, 1955), 98ff.
9. C. S. Lewis, *Out of the Silent Planet* (New York: Macmillan, 1965), 68., 68.
10. W. H. Lewis, ed. *The Letters of C. S. Lewis* (New York: Harcourt, Brace, Jovanovich, 1966), 191.
11. Cf. Lewis, *Mere Christianity*, 54–56; and Lewis, *Miracles*, 109.
12. Lewis, *Miracles*, 48.
13. *Letters of C. S. Lewis*, 233.
14. C. S. Lewis, *The Discarded Image* (Cambridge: Cambridge University Press, 1964), 149–50.
15. Lewis, *Mere Christianity*, 155.
16. Lewis, *Reflections on the Psalms*, 5, 6.
17. *Letters of C. S. Lewis*, 229.
18. C. S. Lewis, *Letters to Malcolm: Chiefly on Prayer* (New York: Harcourt, Brace, Jovanovich, 1963), 70, 71.
19. *Letters of C. S. Lewis*, 201.
20. Ibid., 210.
21. Lewis, *Mere Christianity*, 155.
22. C. S. Lewis, *The Pilgrim's Regress: An Allegorical Apology for Christianity, Reason, and Romanticism* (New York: Bantam, 1933), 192.
23. *Letters of C. S. Lewis*, 191.
24. Lewis, *Reflections on the Psalms*, 133, 134.
25. Lewis, *Mere Christianity*, 186.
26. Lewis, *Letters to Malcolm*, 42.
27. C. S. Lewis, *That Hideous Strength* (New York: Macmillan, 1946), 262.
28. C. S. Lewis, *The Screwtape Letters* (New York: Macmillan, 1961), 8, 9.
29. C. S. Lewis, *Surprised by Joy: The Shape of My Early Life* (New York: Harcourt, Brace, Jovanovich, 1955), 236.

30. C. S. Lewis, *A Grief Observed* (New York: Bantam Books, 1976), 178.

31. Lewis, *Miracles*, 114–15.

32. Lewis, *Mere Christianity*, 155.

33. Ibid., 164.

34. Lewis, *Screwtape Letters*, 148.

35. Martin Moynihan trans. and ed., *The Latin Letters of C. S. Lewis* (South Bend, Ind.: St. Augustines Press, 1998), 60, 61.

36. Lyle W. Dorsett and Marjorie Lamp Mead eds., *C. S. Lewis Letters to Children* (New York, MacMillan, 1985), 85–86.

37. Lewis, *Problem of Pain*, 134.

38. Lewis, *Reflections on the Psalms*, 116.

39. Lewis, *Mere Christianity*, 155.

40. Lewis, *Letters to Malcolm*, 70–71.

41. Lewis, *Miracles*, 113, 114.

42. See Lewis, *Miracles*, 133; Lewis, *Problem of Pain*, 119; and C. S. Lewis, *The Great Divorce* (New York: Macmillan, 1946), 92.

43. Lewis, *Letters to Malcolm*, 85.

44. C. S. Lewis, *The Four Loves* (New York: Harcourt, Brace, Jovanovich, 1960), 177.

45. Lewis, *Miracles*, 51.

46. Lewis, *Mere Christianity*, 57.

47. Lewis, *Miracles*, 130.

48. Lewis, *Screwtape Letters*, 86.

49. Lewis, *Miracles*, 113, 114.

50. Lewis, *Great Divorce*, 46.

51. Lewis, *Miracles*, 111–12.

52. *Letters of C. S. Lewis*, 238.

53. Lewis, *Great Divorce*, 123–24.

54. Lewis, *Screwtape Letters*, 108.

55. *Letters of C. S. Lewis*, 233.

56. Lewis, *Mere Christianity*, 56, 57.

57. Ibid., 155.

58. Lewis, *Miracles*, 145.

59. Ibid., 148, 149.

60. C. S. Lewis, "Miracles," in *God in the Dock: Essays on Theology and Ethics*, ed Walter Hooper (New York: Macmillan, 1970), 35.

61. Lewis, *Great Divorce*, 103–4.

62. C. S. Lewis, *God in the Dock*, 336.

63. C. S. Lewis, *The World's Last Night and Other Essays* (New York: Harcourt, Brace, 1960), 93.

64. Ibid., 94.

65. Ibid., 107.
66. Lewis, *Mere Christianity*, 66.
67. C. S. Lewis, "The Psalms," in *Christian Reflections*, ed. Walter Hooper (Grand Rapids: Eerdman's, 1982), 123.
68. Lewis, *Mere Christianity*, 57.
69. Ibid., 58.
70. *Letters of C. S. Lewis*, 197, 198.
71. Lewis, *Mere Christianity*, 157.
72. Lewis, *Miracles*, 145.
73. C. S. Lewis, *Perelandra* (New York: Macmillan, 1944), 148.
74. Lewis, *Reflections on the Psalms*, 35.
75. Lewis, *Miracles*, 130.
76. *Letters of C. S. Lewis*, 201.
77. W. Norman Pittenger, "Apologist versus Apologist: A Critique of C. S. Lewis as 'Defender of the Faith,' " *Christian Century* (1 October 1958): 1106–7.
78. Lewis, *Problem of Pain*, 134.
79. Lewis, *Mere Christianity*, 143.
80. Ibid., 150. C. S. Lewis, *The Lion, the Witch and the Wardrobe* (New York: MacMillan, 1950), 74, 75.

Conclusion

The Enduring Witness
of C. S. Lewis

We live in a world where, sadly, the majority of people do not believe in Jesus Christ. Many have never really considered the identity and message of Jesus. With preconceptions and prejudices about Christianity, they are reluctant to listen to the church. C. S. Lewis saw this situation and wrote, in part, to answer it. He presented orthodox Christianity in new, translated forms to better reach the modern reader. This work was quite successful.

Through Lewis's writings, many people considered the claims of Jesus and the teachings of Christianity. To this day, his writings continue to have this effect. They continue to present essential, mere Christianity. While Lewis freely speculated about theological details, he also relied on the Christian creeds to summarize the faith. His discussions may involve interesting applications of theology, but his conclusions generally reflect classic, biblical orthodoxy.

LITERARY CHARACTERISTICS

Lewis's theology is unoriginal. He says nothing that is not said by other ancient and modern writers. Still, Lewis's writings remain extremely popular. What is it that makes his writing so effective, and what can we learn from this?

Much of Lewis's effectiveness comes from his writing style and the content of his work. The Christ of Lewis's writings is the Christ of his conversion. Lewis wrote for people who asked the same questions he had asked. His broad and challenging questions resonate with many different readers, and his answers are compelling. Throughout his writings, we have seen four emphases that help explain their effectiveness. First, Lewis presents Christianity in general, and Christ in particular, not as the negation of all other religions, but as the fulfillment of the highest and best religious thought. Second, Lewis presents his theology in clear, simple, and logical terms. Third, he transmits theology through rich, imaginative writing. Finally, his personality enhances the effectiveness of his work.

An essential step in Lewis's conversion was the realization that, while Christianity makes exclusive claims and at times contradicts other religions, this does not negate true elements in other religions. Lewis's own spiritual quest considered the great religions of the world. He concluded that the ethical teachings of Christianity are quite similar to those of other religions. The difference between Christ and other teachers is not the ethical content of their teaching but a difference of person and office. Christ's teaching is similar to that of other great teachers, but He claims to be more than a teacher. He upholds similar ethics, but He also fulfills them in the redemption of the world.

Moreover, and perhaps of greater consequence for Lewis, figures similar to Christ are found in the world's mythologies. Lewis loved mythology, and he saw a clear foreshadowing of Christ in certain myths. For example, he made frequent reference to harvest deities who annually die and rise again. Christ dies and rises just as the Corn-kings, but He is not one further example of this mythology. He is the prototype and the fulfillment that all other expressions reflect. In Christ's incarnation, life, death, and resurrection, myth became fact, and the pagan myths were fulfilled. Christianity is the highest expression of the truth but not the only expression. Lewis does not merely discuss these parallels, he also develops mythological themes and crafts new myths that continue to point to Christ. His prose affirms the usefulness of these genres while his fiction develops them.

A second factor in Lewis's conversion and writing is a focused use of logic. His education emphasized critical thinking, and his acceptance of Christianity included a logical evaluation of its claims. Lewis could not have believed the Christian faith if he were unable to make sense of it. This does not preclude the possibility of the miraculous, mysterious, or supernatural, but a logical coherence was vital. Similarly, Lewis's readers often express an appreciation for his lucid, logical arguments. While he does not address every question, he thoroughly considers the primary claims of Christianity. Lewis ably focuses an issue to a narrow and sharply defined set of alternatives.

As we have noted, Lewis's evaluation of Jesus Christ employs such a precise use of logic. Is it logical to say that Jesus Christ was only a good teacher? No. Because Jesus claimed to be God, He could not merely have been a good teacher. He might have been a liar, a lunatic, or a devil, but it is illogical to call Him simply a good teacher. Lewis repeats this argument several times in his writings, and it is perhaps his best-known logical argument. It is also controversial. Some readers object to its forcefulness. Others argue that there may be other possibilities beyond those Lewis proposes. To present a number of other alternatives, however, requires an expansion of Lewis's presuppositions. The only question under consideration is whether Jesus is merely a good teacher. One may certainly make other assertions, but this does not invalidate Lewis's essential logic. The success of this argument is its simplicity and focus.

Lewis is often commended for his lucidity. Indeed, many have noted that what is most notable in his writings is common sense. This is evident as he approaches the Bible. He was not a biblical literalist and was willing to look at the transmission of Christianity with a critical eye, yet he generally held to the simplest reading of the Scriptures. What the text says is ordinarily what it means. Application may be difficult, but Lewis believed that the need to apply the Bible was obvious. In an era when Christians may be confused by the work of many theologians, this simple acceptance and defense of Christianity is appealing. The teaching may be challenging, but it may also have a greater integrity.

Lewis preferred this straight Christianity to "Christianity and water." Logical argument was vital to his understanding, but Lewis also recognized the limits of human reason. Christianity cannot be figured out simply by experience or logic. It exceeds expectations, and Lewis considered this to be one of its appeals. His presentation of Christianity is logical yet believing, conservative yet intellectual.

A third factor that explains Lewis's effectiveness is his creativity. While some of his work is focused and logical, other aspects of his writing are richly imaginative. This was important in his conversion and his understanding of Christ. Lewis was both personally and professionally immersed in literature. He was a literary critic, a professor, and an excellent storyteller. He had a great love of books, particularly imaginative writings. Lewis freely drew from this rich literary background and incorporated diverse elements in his own stories. Furthermore, Lewis wrote with deliberate complexity and richness. His stories often contain multiple levels of understanding and offer the reader a rewarding depth of meaning.

Lewis's fiction is regarded by many as the high point of his work. His stories do not simply communicate cognitive information. Aslan, Maleldil, Ransom, and Psyche do, indeed, provide information about Christianity to the reader, but their impact exceeds this. The recasting of Christian elements allows the reader to consider anew its claims.

This is not limited to his fiction. Other writings contain shorter illustrations, which likewise use his literary skills, such as his images in *Miracles* (for example, the strongman and the diver) that describe the work of Christ. All Lewis's writings use literary illustrations to explain Christianity.

One final factor that explains Lewis's effectiveness is his personality. His writing is candid and conversational. Readers of Lewis often imagine that they know what he would say about various issues. They have opinions, derived from the tone of his writings, about the sound of his voice. This illusion of knowing Lewis is enhanced by the volumes of correspondence, his autobiographical materials, and recent theatrical and cinematic depictions of his life. Ironically, Lewis would have been uncomfortable with such personal scrutiny. Yet the persona of Lewis shines through his writings.

Personal Characteristics

In addition to literary features, several elements of Lewis's life are particularly relevant to his effectiveness. One of the most significant is the fact that Lewis was a convert to Christianity. He had been an atheist, but when he examined the evidence for Christianity, he felt that it was the only logical choice. An examination of its claims led him to believe the truthfulness of the Christian faith. The fruits of this conversion are evident in his writings. Lewis wrote what he thought and experienced. His writings address common objections to Christianity that he himself once raised. After discovering answers to his questions, Lewis repeats the questions and offers the answers for his readers. What emerges is a genuine consideration of some widely asked questions coupled with solutions that have satisfied many.

Additionally, this convert who wrote about his own experience also wrote as an individual Christian. Lewis was a layman, an "outsider" with no financial stake in what he was writing. He did not earn his living from his theological writing but from his professorship in a secular field. While a critic may discount the work of a clergyman or professional theologian as part of his career, Lewis did not rely on his theological writing for his support. He was, indeed, a remarkably well-educated layman. He demonstrates a familiarity with biblical Greek and with primary theological sources. When Lewis explains theology to his readers, it is obvious that he understands that theology.

Closely related to this is Lewis's ecumenicity. He repeatedly stated that his intention was to focus on the teachings held in common by the majority of Christians. This is a particularly notable theme in *Mere Christianity*. Lewis was an Anglican, but he was neither ordained nor employed by the church. When he wrote of common Christian teachings, his readers believed him. It might be argued that his foundation in Anglicanism, with its historic emphasis on central Christian teaching, encouraged this focus on common doctrine. At the same time, his personal life experiences may have contributed to this ecumenical interest. Lewis was born in Northern Ireland and knew well the division between Protestants and Roman Catholics. While echoes of this antagonism sometimes appear in his writings, Lewis truly sought common ground. Additionally, his friends included people of diverse religious backgrounds. Readers from many denominations find common ground in Lewis's expression of Christianity.

Another aspect of Lewis's personality that enhances his reception is his intelligence. Lewis's work is unique, and it is deep.

Lewis may write about theological issues, but he speaks in scientific, literary, and cultural terms. He refers to a variety of sources, assuming the reader will be familiar with them. The reader is treated with integrity and respect.

Yet another facet of Lewis's personality is his honesty. His works reveal a man who struggled with life's difficult issues. He was not merely a writer but a regular person with his own trials and struggles. His personal history, as well as his writings, reveals a man who tried to apply his faith. This genuine struggle adds credibility and integrity to his work.

Lewis's effectiveness, then, may be ascribed to a variety of factors. Without belittling other religions, he holds to the integrity and truth of Christianity. His approach is clear and logical but also imaginative. His writings are honest, reflecting his own experiences and ideas. Lewis has the breadth of knowledge to see the fulfillment of pagan mythology and non-Christian religions. He is simultaneously logical and imaginative, scholarly and devotional, impressive and unassuming. His writings embrace diverse methods and genres. Consequently, while it is unusual to find a reader who appreciates all of Lewis's writing, one rarely finds a reader who dislikes it all. Lewis's use of diverse elements allows him to reach a wide audience.

WEAKNESSES OF C. S. LEWIS

The books of C. S. Lewis present a broad range of material, from direct discourse and explanation to fiction, children's stories, and mythology. Beyond these varied works, he also wrote significant books within his academic field. Still, there are weaknesses and inadequacies in his writing that should be considered.

Perhaps the chief weakness in Lewis's theological writings was also one of his strengths. Lewis was a layman. While that provided him with an enhanced sense of objectivity, it also adversely affected his writing. Although Lewis was well read in theology, he was untrained. Consequently, his theological writing is, at times, imprecise and has led some readers to suspect heresy. At other times, his writings are precise but awkward. Additionally, while his use of fictional and mythical forms richly conveys his theological thought, they are equally prone to misapplication and misinterpretation. Stories may communicate on a deeper level than direct discourse, but they offer unique challenges to any author. It is difficult to express one's theology precisely without resorting to allegory. As Lewis strongly resisted allegorical writing, his fiction may not communicate theologically with the clarity of his other writing. These weaknesses are understandable, but they remain weaknesses.

Second, while some readers are strongly attracted by Lewis's use of common-sense logic, many critics have disputed his arguments. He is frequently accused of using questionable dichotomies, reducing an argument to two narrow possibilities while ignoring other valid positions. Likewise, he is accused of simplistic reasoning, dismissing a counterargument too easily. His logical constructs are highly focused, but that is not always apparent to the reader. Some readers may easily dismiss an argument that appeared solid to Lewis.

Third, Lewis's writings may be less effective today because of the passage of time. Certain material and allusions within them are less significant today than when first written. His use of now-outdated embryology in *Mere Christianity* illustrates this. The point he makes, that Christ humbled Himself, is appropriate. The usefulness of the illustration, however, has diminished with time. Similar situations may exist within his writings. Frequent references to World War II were certainly appropriate when first written, but they are far less effective with younger readers. Some of Lewis's books are showing their age.

Finally, his focus on mere Christianity, the teachings held in common by all Christians, may lead to criticism. Which Christian teachings really are essential and held in common by all Christians? Some people object to the absence of certain doctrines. Others may note that, while Lewis claims to restrict himself to common Christian teachings, he strays from this ideal. Teachings of purgatory and prayer for the dead are not held by all Christians, yet both topics are addressed within Lewis's writings. These objections are a symptom of a divided Christendom, but they are significant.

THE LEGACY OF C. S. LEWIS

C. S. Lewis took up the task of communicating essential Christian teaching to the ordinary person. While his presentation of Christology has weak points, it is, nonetheless, largely successful. Nearly 40 years after his death, almost all of Lewis's writings remain in print and continue to sell at a rapid pace. Despite his stated intent, Lewis is now largely read as a theologian and will likely remain a popular theologian for quite some time.

While this may be positive, it is not without negative consequences. The success of Lewis has made it nearly inevitable that those who write popular Christian books will be compared to him. Many people are watching for the "next C. S. Lewis" but to no avail. Attempts to produce writers who emulate Lewis's writings will not produce the spontaneity or depth of writing that Lewis achieved. If he had used one model as a standard for his work, he would not have written the variety of books that he did. It was his willingness and eagerness to work with new forms and narratives that led to his outstanding writing. Modern writers should not be encouraged simply to emulate one past writer but to write new material.

Nor should emulation of Lewis's writing consist of simple adherence to the forms or styles he used. Yet he may be seen as a paradigm for popular theology because of his willingness to present orthodox theology in new language and in diverse forms. The need for translated theology is as vital today as when Lewis began his work. Above all, our world needs to hear about Jesus Christ.

Lewis was once asked to respond in writing to the question, "What are we to make of Jesus Christ?" He answered by restating his logical evaluation of Jesus' claims. At the beginning and end of his essay, however, he remarked that "the real question is not what are we to make of Christ but what is He to make of us?"[1] This is Lewis's Christology. He clearly and creatively presents the biblical Christ. We are not God, but Christ is. He is in control. Yet the untamable Son of God willingly humbled Himself to be our Savior. So Lewis describes his most famous Christ figure,

> "Aslan is a lion—*the* Lion, the great Lion." ...
>
> "Then he isn't safe?" ...
>
> "Who said anything about safe? 'Course he isn't safe. But he's good. He's the King, I tell you."[2]

Neither Aslan nor Christ is "safe" by human standards. Neither is tamed or controlled by human beings. But Christ is good, and He tames Himself to be our Savior.

NOTES

1. C. S. Lewis, "What Are We to Make of Jesus Christ," in *God in the Dock: Essays on Theology and Ethics*, ed Walter Hooper (New York: Macmillan, 1970), 156.

2. C. S. Lewis, *The Lion, the Witch and the Wardrobe* (New York: MacMillan, 1950), 75, 76.

Appendix

A Chronology of the Life and Works of C. S. Lewis

1898
(November 29) Born in Belfast

CA. **1903**
(Age 5) Begins writing *Boxen*

CA. **1904**
Names self "Jacksie"

1905
Moves to "New House" in the country ("Little Lea")

1908
(August 23) Mother dies—sent to boarding school
Wynyard School, Hertford-shire

1910
Campbell College, Belfast

1911
Malvern Preparatory School

1913
Malvern College, Worcester

1914–1916
Studies with tutor W. T. Kirk-patrick ("The Great Knock") in Surrey

CA. **1915**
Reads *Phantastes*

1917
Begins study at University College, Oxford
World War I interrupts Oxford studies
(November) Arrives on the front lines

1918
Hospitalized once for trench fever and again after being wounded
Discharged from army

1919
(January) Returns to Oxford as student
Spirits in Bondage (pseudonym: Clive Hamilton)

1920
Takes a First in Classical Mod-erations

1922
Takes a First in Greats

1923
Takes a First in English Lan-guage and Literature

1924
Becomes substitute tutor in philosophy, University Col-lege, Oxford

1925

Elected tutor of English language and literature at Magdalen College, Oxford

1926

Dymer (pseudonym: Clive Hamilton)
Meets J. R. R. Tolkien

1929

Trinity Term: conversion to theism
(September 25) Father dies

1931

(Late summer) writes that he has accepted Christianity

1933

Pilgrim's Regress

1936

Allegory of Love
Meets Charles Williams

1938

Out of the Silent Planet

1939

Evacuated children arrive at the Kilns
The Personal Heresy

1940

First weekly Inklings meeting
The Problem of Pain

1941

Four Radio Talks (later compiled into *Mere Christianity*)

1942

Preface to Paradise Lost
The Screwtape Letters
Broadcast Talks/The Case for Christianity

1943

Gives Riddell Memorial Lectures (become *The Abolition of Man*)
Perelandra
Christian Behaviour

1945

That Hideous Strength
The Great Divorce
Beyond Personality
Charles Williams dies

1946

Awarded doctor of divinity degree, *honoris causa*, St. Andrew's University

1947

Miracles
(September 8) Lewis on cover of *Time*

1948

Mrs. Moore enters nursing home, and Lewis visits daily
Arthurian Torso

1949

Transposition and Other Addresses

1950

The Lion, the Witch and the Wardrobe

1951

Mrs. Moore dies
Prince Caspian

1952

Doctor of letters, *honoris causa*, L'université Laval, Quebec
Mere Christianity
The Voyage of the Dawn Treader
Joy visits

1953

The Silver Chair

1954

English Literature in the Six-teenth Century (Excluding Drama)
The Horse and His Boy
Elected professor of medieval and renaissance literature at Magdalene College, Cambridge
Joy moves to England

1955

Surprised by Joy
Magician's Nephew

1956

Till We Have Faces
The Last Battle
(April 23) Civil marriage to Joy
Joy diagnosed with cancer

1957

(March 21) Christian marriage to Joy
(Midyear) Joy's cancer in remission

1958

Reflections on the Psalms

1959

Elected honorary fellow of University College, Oxford
Doctor of letters, Manchester University
Joins Bishop's Commission for Revision of the Psalter
Joy's cancer returns

1960

The Four Loves
Studies in Words
The World's Last Night and Other Essays
(July 13) Joy dies

1961

A Grief Observed (pseudonym: N. W. Clerk)
An Experiment in Criticism

1962

They Asked for a Paper

1963

(November 22) Lewis dies

POSTHUMOUSLY PUBLISHED WORKS
All My Road before Me
Boxen
The Dark Tower and Other Stories
The Discarded Image
Letters to Malcolm: Chiefly on Prayer
Spenser's Images of Life
Various collections of essays and letters

Selected Bibliography

PRIMARY SOURCES

Lewis, Clive Staples. *The Abolition of Man: How Education Develops Man's Sense of Morality*. New York: Collier, 1947.

———. *All My Road before Me: The Diary of C. S. Lewis 1922–1927*. Edited by Walter Hooper. London: Harcourt, Brace, Jovanovich, 1991.

———. *The Allegory of Love: A Study in Medieval Tradition*. Oxford: Clarendon, 1936.

———. *An Experiment in Criticism*. Cambridge: Cambridge University Press, 1961.

———, and Charles Williams. *Arthurian Torso: Containing the Posthumous Fragment of the Figure of Arthur by Charles Williams and a Commentary on the Arthurian Poems of Charles Williams by C. S. Lewis*. Grand Rapids: Eerdmans, 1974.

———. *Boxen: The Imaginary World of the Young C. S. Lewis*. Edited by Walter Hooper. New York: Harcourt, Brace, Jovanovich, 1985.

———. *Christian Reflections*. Edited by Walter Hooper. Grand Rapids: Eerdmans, 1982.

———. *Collected Letters Volume 1: Family Letters 1905–1931*. Edited by Walter Hooper. London: HarperCollins, 2000.

———. *The Collected Poems of C. S. Lewis*. Edited by Walter Hooper. London: Fount Paper Backs, 1994.

———. *The Dark Tower and Other Stories*. Edited by Walter Hooper. New York: Harcourt, Brace, Jovanovich, 1977.

———. *The Discarded Image*. Cambridge: Cambridge University Press, 1964.

———. *Dymer*. New York: Macmillan, 1950.

———. *English Literature in the Sixteenth Century Excluding Drama*. Volume Three of *The Oxford History of English Literature*. Oxford: Clarendon, 1954.

———, ed. *Essays Presented to Charles Williams*. Grand Rapids: Eerdmans, 1966.

———. *Fern-Seed and Elephants and Other Essays on Christianity*. Edited, with a preface by Walter Hooper. London: Collins-Fontana Books, 1975.

———. *An Experiment in Criticism*. New York: Cambridge University Press, 1961.

———. *The Four Loves*. New York: Harcourt, Brace, Jovanovich, 1960.

———. *God in the Dock: Essays on Theology and Ethics*. Edited by Walter Hooper. New York: Macmillan, 1970.

———. *The Great Divorce*. New York: Macmillan, 1946.

———. *A Grief Observed*. New York: Bantam, 1976.

———. *The Horse and His Boy*. New York: Macmillan, 1954.

———. *The Last Battle*. New York: Macmillan, 1956.

———. *The Latin Letters of C. S. Lewis*. Translated and edited by Martin Moynihan. South Bend, Ind.: St. Augustine's Press, 1998.

———. *Letters of C. S. Lewis*. Edited by W. H. Lewis. New York: Harvest/ Harcourt, Brace, Jovanovich, 1966.

———. *Letters to an American Lady*. Edited by Clyde S. Kilby. Grand Rapids: Eerdmans, 1967.

———. *Letters to Children*. Edited by Lyle W. Dorsett and Marjorie Lamp Mead. New York: Macmillan, 1985.

———. *Letters to Malcolm, Chiefly on Prayer*. New York: Macmillan, 1964.

———. *The Lion, the Witch and the Wardrobe*. New York: Macmillan, 1950.

———. *The Magician's Nephew*. New York: Macmillan, 1955.

———. *Mere Christianity*. New York: Macmillan, 1952.

———. *Miracles: A Preliminary Study*. New York: Macmillan, 1947.

———. *Narrative Poems*. Edited by Walter Hooper. London: Fount Paperbacks, 1969.

———. *Of Other Worlds: Essays and Stories*. Edited by Walter Hooper. London: Geoffrey Bles, 1966.

———. *On Stories and Other Essays on Literature*. Edited by Walter Hooper. New York: Harcourt, Brace, Jovanovich, 1982.

———. *Out of the Silent Planet*. New York: Macmillan, 1965.

———. *Perelandra: A Novel*. New York: Macmillan, 1944.

———, and E. M. W. Tillyard. *The Personal Heresy: A Controversy*. London: Oxford University Press, 1939.

———. *The Pilgrim's Regress: An Allegorical Apology for Christianity, Reason, and Romanticism*. New York: Bantam, 1933.

———. *Prince Caspian: The Return to Narnia*. New York: Macmillan, 1951.

———. *A Preface to Paradise Lost*. Oxford: Oxford University Press, 1942.

———. *The Problem of Pain*. New York: Macmillan, 1962.

———. *Reflections on the Psalms*. New York: Harcourt, Brace, Jovanovich, 1958.

———. *Rehabilitations and Other Essays*. London: Oxford University Press, 1939.

———. *The Screwtape Letters*. New York: Macmillan, 1961.

———. *Selected Literary Essays*. Edited, with a preface by Walter Hooper. Cambridge: Cambridge University Press, 1969.

———. *The Silver Chair*. New York: Macmillan, 1953.

———. *Spenser's Images of Life*. Edited by Alastair Fowler. Cambridge: Cambridge University Press, 1967.

———. *Spirits in Bondage: A Cycle of Lyrics*. New York: Harvest/HBJ, 1984.

———. *Studies in Medieval and Renaissance Literature*. Edited by Walter Hooper. Cambridge: Cambridge University Press, 1966.

———. *Studies in Words*. Cambridge: Canto, 1991.

———. *Surprised by Joy: The Shape of My Early Life*. New York: Harcourt, Brace, Jovanovich, 1955.

———. *That Hideous Strength: A Modern Fairy-Tale for Grown-ups*. New York: Macmillan, 1946.

———. *They Asked for a Paper: Papers and Addresses*. London: Geofrey Bles, 1962.

———. *They Stand Together: The Letters of C. S. Lewis to Arthur Greeves (1914–1963)*. Edited by Walter Hooper. London: Collins, 1979.

———. *Till We Have Faces*. New York: Harcourt, Brace, Jovanovich, 1956.

———. *The Voyage of the Dawn Treader*. New York: Macmillan, 1952.

———. *The Weight of Glory and Other Addresses*. Grand Rapids: Eerdmans, 1949.

———. *The World's Last Night and Other Essays*. New York: Harcourt Brace, & Co., 1960.

———, ed. *George MacDonald: An Anthology*. New York: Macmillan, 1947.

SELECTED SECONDARY SOURCES

Aulén, Gustav. *Christus Victor: An Historical Study of the Three Main Types of the Atonement*. Translated by A. G. Hiebert. New York, Macmillan, 1969.

Barfield, Owen. *Poetic Diction: A Study in Meaning*. Hanover, N.H.: University Press of New England, 1973.

Beversluis, John. *C. S. Lewis and the Search for Rational Religion*. Grand Rapids: Eerdmans, 1985.

Carnell, Corbin S. *Bright Shadow of Reality: C. S. Lewis and the Feeling Intellect*. Grand Rapids: Eerdmans, 1974.

Carpenter, Humphrey. *The Inklings*. New York: Ballantine, 1978.

Christopher, Joe R., and Joan K. Ostling. *C. S. Lewis: An Annotated Checklist of Writings about Him and His Works*. Kent, Ohio: Kent State University Press, n.d.

"Commission on Revision of Psalter: Translation Errors to be Removed." *Times* (London), 28 November 1969, 6c.

Coren, Michael. *The Man Who Created Narnia: The Story of C. S. Lewis*. Grand Rapids: Eerdmans, 1996.

Cunningham, Richard B. *C. S. Lewis, Defender of the Faith*. Philadelphia: Westminster, 1967.

"Don v. Devil." *Time* 50, 8 September 1947, 65–66, 68, 71–72.

Douglas, J. D. "The Legacy of C. S. Lewis." *Christianity Today* 8 (20 December 1963): 27.

Duriez, Colin. *The C. S. Lewis Handbook: A Comprehensive Guide to His Life, Thought, and Writings*. Grand Rapids: Baker, 1990.

Ford, Paul F. *Companion to Narnia: A Complete Guide to the Themes, Characters, and Events of C. S. Lewis's Enchanting Imaginary World*. New York: Collier, 1986.

Frazer, James George. *The Golden Bough*. New York: Macmillan, 1922.

Freshwater, Mark Edwards. *C. S. Lewis and the Truth of Myth*. Lanham, Md.: University Press of America, 1988.

Gibb, Jocelyn. *Light on C. S. Lewis*. New York: Harcourt, Brace, Jovanovich, 1976.

Gibson, Evan K. *C. S. Lewis, Spinner of Tales: A Guide to His Fiction*. Washington D.C.: Christian College Press, 1980.

Gilbert, Douglas, and Clyde S. Kilby. *C. S. Lewis: Images of His World*. Grand Rapids: Eerdmans, 1973.

Glover, Donald D. *C. S. Lewis: The Art of Enchantment*. Athens, Ohio: Ohio University Press, 1981.

Goffar, Janine. *C. S. Lewis Index: Rumours from the Sculptor's Shop*. Riverside, Calif.: La Sierra University Press, 1995.

Green, Roger Lancelyn, and Walter Hooper. *C. S. Lewis: A Biography*. New York: Harcourt, Brace, Jovanovich, 1974.

Griffin, William. *Clive Staples Lewis: A Dramatic Life*. San Francisco: Harper & Row, 1986.

Holmer, Paul L. *C. S. Lewis: The Shape of His Faith and Thought*. New York: Harper & Row, 1976.

Hooper, Walter. *C. S. Lewis: A Companion and Guide*. New York: Harper-Collins, 1996.

———. *Past Watchful Dragons*. New York: Collier, 1971.

Howard, Thomas. *The Achievement of C. S. Lewis*. Wheaton: Harold Shaw, 1980.

———. *C. S. Lewis: Man of Letters: a Reading of His Fiction*. San Francisco: Ignatius Press, 1987.

Huttar, Charles A., and Peter J. Schakel, eds. *Word and Story in C. S. Lewis*. Colombia: University of Missouri Press, 1991.

Junes, Carla Faust. "The Literary Detective Computer Analysis of Stylistic Differences between *The Dark Tower* and C. S. Lewis' Deep Space Trilogy." *Mythlore* 15.3 (Spring 1989): 11–15.

Karkainen, Paul A. *Narnia Explored*. Old Tappan, N.J.: Fleming H. Revell, 1979.

Keefe, Carolyn, ed. *C. S. Lewis: Speaker and Teacher*. Grand Rapids: Zondervan, 1971.

Kilby, Clyde S., and M. C. Mead. *Brothers and Friends: The Diaries of Major Warren Hamilton Lewis*. San Francisco: Harper & Row, 1982.

Kilby, Clyde S. *The Christian World of C. S. Lewis*. Grand Rapids: Eerdmans, 1964.

———. *Images of Salvation in the Fiction of C. S. Lewis*. Wheaton: Harold Shaw, 1978.

Lindskoog, Kathryn. *C. S. Lewis: Mere Christian*. Revised and expanded. Downers Grove, Ill.: Intervarsity Press, 1981.

————. *The Lion of Judah in Never-Never Land: The Theology of C. S. Lewis Expressed in His Fantasies for Children*. Grand Rapids: Eerdmans, 1973.

————. *Sleuthing Lewis: More Light in the Shadowlands*. Macon, Ga.: Mercer University Press, 2001.

Loades, Ann. "C. S. Lewis: Grief Observed, Rationality Abandoned, Faith Regained." *Journal of Literature and Theology* 3.1 (March 1989): 107–21.

Lowenberg, Susan. *C. S. Lewis: A Reference Guide 1972–1988*. New York: G. K. Hall, 1993.

MacDonald, George. *Phantastes: A Faerie Romance*. Grand Rapids: Eerdmans, 1981.

McLaughlin, Sara Park, and Mark O. Webb. *A Word Index to the Poetry of C. S. Lewis*. West Cornwall, Conn.: Locust Hill, 1988.

Meilaender, Gilbert. *The Taste for the Other: The Social and Ethical Thought of C. S. Lewis*. Grand Rapids: Eerdmans, 1978.

Menuge, Angus, ed. *C. S. Lewis: Lightbearer in the Shadowlands: The Evangelistic Vision of C. S. Lewis*. Wheaton: Crossways, 1997.

Montgomery, John W., ed. *Myth, Allegory and Gospel: An Interpretation of J. R. R. Tolkien, C. S. Lewis, G. K. Chesterton [and] Charles Williams*. Minneapolis: Bethany Fellowship, 1974.

Moorman, Charles. *Arthurian Triptych: Mythic Materials in Charles Williams, C. S. Lewis, and T. S. Eliot*. Berkeley: University of California Press, 1960.

Payne, Leanne. *Real Presence: The Christian Worldview of C. S. Lewis as Incarnational Reality*. Revised edition. Westchester, Ill.: Crossway Books, 1988.

Pittenger, W. Norman. "Apologist versus Apologist: A Critique of C. S. Lewis as 'Defender of the Faith.' " *Christian Century* 75 (1 October 1958): 1104–7.

Purtill, Richard L. *C. S. Lewis's Case for the Christian Faith*. San Francisco: Harper & Row, 1981.

————. *Lord of the Elves and Eldils: Fantasy and Philosophy in C. S. Lewis and J. R. R. Tolkien*. Grand Rapids: Zondervan, 1974.

Rose, Mary Carman. "The Christian Platonism of C. S. Lewis, J. R. R. Tolkien, and Charles Williams." In *Neoplatonism and Christian Thought*, edited by Dominic J. O'Meara. Norfolk, Va.: International Society for Neoplatonic Studies, 1981.

Rossow, Francis C. "Echoes of the Gospel-Event in Literature and Elsewhere." *Concordia Journal* 9.2 (March 1983): 50–58.

Sammons, Martha C. *A Guide through Narnia*. Wheaton: Harold Shaw, 1979.

Sayer, George. *Jack: C. S. Lewis and His Times*. San Francisco: Harper & Row, 1988.

Sayers, Dorothy L. "The Writing and Reading of Allegory." In *The Poetry of Search and the Poetry of Statement, and Other Posthumous Essays on Literature, Religion, and Language*. London, Victor Gollacz, 1963.

Schakel, Peter J., ed. *The Longing for a Form: Essays on the Fiction of C. S. Lewis*. Kent, Ohio: Kent State University Press, 1977.

———. *Reading with the Heart: The Way into Narnia*. Grand Rapids: Eerdmans, 1979.

———. *Reason and Imagination in C. S. Lewis: A Study of* Till We Have Faces. Grand Rapids: Eerdmans, 1994.

Smith, Robert Houston. *Patches of Godlight: The Pattern of Thought in C. S. Lewis*. Athens, Ga.: University of Georgia Press, 1981.

Taliaferro, Charles A. "A Narnian Theory of the Atonement." *Scottish Journal of Theology* 41.1 (1988): 75–92.

Urang, Gunnar. *Shadows of Heaven: Religion and Fantasy in the Writing of C. S. Lewis, Charles Williams, and J. R. R. Tolkien*. Philadelphia: Pilgrim Press, 1971.

Walsh, Chad. *C. S. Lewis: Apostle to the Skeptics*. New York: Macmillan, 1949.

———. *The Literary Legacy of C. S. Lewis*. New York: Harcourt, Brace, Jovanovich, 1979.